Praise for *French Lessons*

" Alice Kaplan beautifully describes the intricate mixture of lust and embarrassment and voyeurism and submission and pride involved in immersing oneself in another language. . . . This girl's own story—of a daughter, a spy in the house of French, a teacher and scholar—is imbued with a sense of the multiplicity of identity, and it gracefully tells us what Kaplan says French has taught her: 'There is more than one way to speak.' "
—Lisa Cohen, *Voice Literary Supplement*

"An uncommonly forthright and concise piece of autobiography. Kaplan has shown that university professors, too, can have a past worth telling, that the subjects they teach may mean far more to them than any student could begin to guess."
—John Sturrock, *London Review of Books*

"This original, artful, engaging book belongs to an evolving genre of postmodern intellectual autobiography. Telling her story about a girl from the midwest who learned to speak perfect French, a student of deconstruction who became intrigued by fascism, Alice Kaplan writes insightfully also about language, memory, politics, and writing. Kaplan's father was a lawyer at the Nuremberg trials who died when she was only seven: she recalls the frightening photographs of concentration camp victims she found among his papers. The glamour of otherness and the allure of evil—as well as the characters of various mentors, meals, lovers, and students—are the subjects of this witty and insightful memoir."
—Rachel M. Brownstein, author of *Becoming a Heroine*

"Born a Jewish daughter of the American Midwest, Alice Kaplan became a professor of French and an expert on the literature of French fascism. *French Lessons* is the story of her cultural odyssey, a brave attempt to articulate the compulsions that drove her to embrace foreignness in order to become truly herself. . . . Told in a 'staccato Midwestern style,' her story of becoming French is arrestingly all-American."
—Arthur Goldhammer, *Washington Post Book World*

"Alice Kaplan has written a wonderful book, as accessible as light fiction and as polished and layered as poetry. . . . The precision and intensity of Kaplan's presentation of self in everyday life makes for an extraordinary literary achievement."
—Graham Fraser, *Toronto Globe and Mail*

"A lovely book. . . . From the childhood learning of words from her siblings, to her professorship at Duke, she has catalogued her desire to speak a foreign language and thereby to become something foreign and alluring herself."
—Fred Turner, *Boston Phoenix*

"*French Lessons* captures the excitement Kaplan experienced as she fell into the French language: mastering the difficulties of French pronunciation, the forms of the French verb, the forms of French politeness."
—Thomas McGonigle, *Chicago Tribune*

"This is the most engaging new *bildungsroman* I have read in years—and especially because the *bildung* in question, the learning of French by a young American woman, brings with it such an amazing range of personal drama of modern and contemporary political and cultural history."
—R. W. B. Lewis

French Lessons

French

Alice Kaplan

Lessons

A Memoir

The University of Chicago Press

Chicago and London

For David

The University of Chicago Press, Chicago 60637
The University of Chicago Press, Ltd., London
© 1993 by The University of Chicago
All rights reserved. Published 1993
Paperback edition 1994
Printed in the United States of America
02 01 00 99 98 97 96   7 8 9 10 11 12
ISBN: 0-226-42418-9 (cloth)
ISBN: 0-226-42419-7 (paper)

Library of Congress Cataloging-in-Publication Data
Kaplan, Alice Yaeger.
    French lessons : a memoir / Alice Kaplan.
        p.   cm.
    1. Kaplan, Alice Yaeger.   2. French teachers—United States—
Biography.   3. French philology—Study and teaching—United States.
I. Title.
PC2064.K36A3   1993
448'.0071'173—dc20
[B]   93-649
                                                        CIP

The paper used in this publication meets the minimum
requirements of the American National Standard for
Information Sciences—Permanence of Paper for Printed
Library Materials, ANSI Z39.48-1984.

After all, that is, everybody who writes is interested
in living inside themselves in order to tell what is
inside themselves. That is why writers have to have
two countries, the one where they belong and the one
in which they live really. The second one is romantic,
it is separate from themselves, it is not real but it is
really there.

—Gertrude Stein, *Paris France* (1940)

When my younger sister came back from France
the first time she had clothes
and perfume that swept the house
as if she had come upon
a stolen treasure all at once.

Her face was a movie
star's, the thin line
of her eyebrows traced the delicate
script of Europe,
unreadable to us.

She could no longer find words
for common things
and uncommon emotions,
she maintained, were best left
in the original.

—Linda Orr, from "Her Visits," in *A Certain X* (1980)

Contents

Part One: *Before I Knew French*

First Words

"Let's get her to say it." My sister was ambitious for me.
"She's only three." My brother was the skeptic.
"Come on, I think she can do it. Come on!"
"All right, all right, let's see if she can do it."
"OK, repeat after us: 'Everything I like is.'"
"EverythingIlike is."
And on it went, ending with the three big words: "illegal," "immoral," and "fattening."

Getting my sister and brother's attention, winning a place in their games, was the biggest challenge. In an ideal world, my sister would let me sit on her bed when her friend Jane came over. My brother would let me watch Perry Mason with him; together we would guess who did it. I couldn't believe my luck when they decided to teach me a saying. The two of them together! The saying was immortalized on a piece of knotty pine one of them had brought back from camp: "Everything I like is either illegal, immoral, or fattening." The words were burned on the wood with a special tool you got to use in crafts class. The words were written, not just printed, with curlicues on the ends of letters, and a flourish underneath.

I didn't know what "illegal" meant. I didn't know what "immoral" meant. I had a clue about "fattening," but I didn't know what it had to do with "illegal" and "immoral." I figured if I could learn to say it, my brother and sister would let me in on other games. "Everything I like is either illegal, immoral, or fattening. Everything I like is either illegal immoral or fattening." I said it again and again until I was dizzy and all the words dissolved into one word, "everythingilikeiseitherillegalimmoralorfattening."

"Not bad." They had a glint in their eye.

My parents gathered around. I performed the sentence for them, with my brother and sister standing proudly by. My father laughed loudest.

It was the biggest language thrill produced in the house since my brother had learned the Tom Lehrer song "Fight Fiercely Harvard" and explained to his elementary school teacher that a football was a spheroid. ("Throw that spheroid down the field and fight! fight! fight!") The teacher had called home to report my brother's astonishing vocabulary.

"Well kids, let's hope it doesn't turn out to be true." My mother made the exit line so she could get started on dinner. The rest of them scattered.

I was left standing in the living room, contemplating my success. Daddy laughed. He understood. What a miracle. I didn't even understand the sentence and it still worked! My father looked just the way he looked when other adults came over for dinner and they talked in the living room after dinner, and he would lean back in his wing chair with his legs crossed, and guffaw. I amused him, as if I were a grownup. All it took was saying grownup words.

When I started to talk on my own, I couldn't be stopped.

When I was in first grade, my sister's friends could hardly stand to ride to school with me in the car. I was loud and unrelenting. I liked to run my own bath water while I sang the song of the rest of my life, endless verses with my own lyrics: I would rule the world, I would sing on a stage, I would travel the seas. My father liked to listen to me sing.

Listening now to my childhood as the French professor I've become, what I hear first are scenes of language. Two Yiddish words came down to me from hearing my mother talk on the phone with her Jewish friends. She used a word for incompetency, "shlemiel," and a word for wild nonsensical ideas, "mishegossen." I heard just enough Yiddish in childhood to imagine a world of awkward, foolish people with wild plans that turned to buffoonery. Yiddish sounds, in and of themselves, were tempting, full of vulgar but thrilling possibilities, like "oy" with its diphthong you could stretch in your mouth for as long or short as you wanted. My grandmother, Ethel Yaeger, had a longer version of "oy": "oy vey ist mir." She mumbled it under her breath. There was also "Gesundheit—ist besser wie krankeit," a ritual sentence she used if one of us sneezed ("it's better than sickness"). There was "Gut in himmel," part acknowledgment of the power of God, part anger at whatever inconvenience He had caused.

The words stuck out too much for me to use at Northrop Collegiate, the private girls' school I had gone to since kindergarten. They made me feel funny, "oy" especially. "Oy" was in the same category as swear words, satisfying and ugly. I liked to say it to myself. "Wherever did you learn to say that," my mother asked, in mock shock, when I punctuated a sentence with "oy." When I got to college I heard people "oying" and "oy veying" with great ease, loud and clear. They sounded brazen to me.

I grew up half a block from a city lake in an old Minneapolis neighborhood populated by prosperous Republicans with names like "Colby" and "Dorsey" and "White." My parents hadn't migrated with others of their generation to the middle-class Jewish suburb, St. Louis Park, because my father wanted to be near a lake. Our house had been built in 1914 for people with servants. There were front stairs and back stairs, a bell button buried in the dining room floor, and on the wall of the dining room, an English hunting scene. There was an eight-burner restaurant stove with a griddle for pancakes, and a butler's pantry with the cupboards painted cream outside and mandarin red inside. There were five bedrooms and a library for my father, and a clothes chute, and a separate garage with a big lilac tree, and a rock garden for my mother. She had a garden smock and gloves and would climb around out there while my father was at work. In the spring the lilac bloomed and the smell came into our house, the smell of our prosperity.

The previous owners had left a set of papers on the radiator in the dining room, which my parents found the day they moved in. It was a detective's report assuring the old owners that although we were Jews, our general comportment was in line with the gentility of the neighborhood. Was the seller stupid enough to leave the report by mistake, or did he want us to see it and to understand our social responsibilities? Did it prove that we belonged there, that we were the "exception"? This episode sat in the back of my mind as I grew up. I watched us. We were on trial, being upright for the neighborhood.

We were so American. It seems now that no one will ever again have that sense of being American that we had then, in the time between the Second World War and Vietnam. It was the time of our father's success and our growing up.

We spoke American in that house: I can't reproduce this language, but I know exactly what I mean by it. It was American more for what we talked about than how it sounded, although it is amazing to think that in one generation, a language could become so native, so comfortable, so normal, with no sense whatever of its relative newness: my parents were, after all, the first ones in their families to be born into English.

"Mom, why did you only go out with Jewish boys?"

"My god, I didn't even think about it. That was our world, we had no choice. You've got to understand, things were very different then. At Douglas School they said that Jews smelled like garlic. We Jewish students sat together in grade school, in high school, and at the University of Minnesota. Why, we even had our own table at the library. It was so limiting!"

The world had kept her at one table in the library. She wanted our world to be different.

My mother still corrects my English grammar, in speech and in writing: "'to whom,' not 'to who'"; "'effective,' not 'affective'"; "'he did well,' but 'he is good.'" She corrects the number of times I use "very." She is against waste in language. Her sentences are short and blunt, yet ripe with innuendo and the promise that more is being said than meets the ear. Now I write in the staccato Midwestern style she taught me.

I could depend on each of my parents to utter fixed expressions in certain circumstances. My father brought the law home from work. "Don't make a federal case out of it," he would say. My mother would say—an expression from around town, Irish maybe—"the jig is up!" When she and I would come home from shopping for shoes, or a winter coat, or a new school uniform, she'd open the back door of the house and peek around the corner into the kitchen and pronounce us "home again, Finnegan." I liked the satisfying sounds, the click of the words over her palate, in "jig" and "Finnegan." conformity?

Our dinner table was the place to learn language etiquette: what to say, what rhythm, when to step in, when to keep out. Our table was civil and civic. Dinner was at the same time every night, and it took forty-five minutes. Levine Blue served the meal in time to get the last bus home to the north side of town, where my father had grown up in a Jewish neighborhood, now a black neighborhood separated from us by a freeway. My father sat at the head of the table with his back to the kitchen door, still in his work suit, brown, light brown shoes with the little holes up by the toe. My sister was across the table from my father, eating fast so she would be excused early. I was next to my mother and across the table from my brother. My brother and I were fighting under the table with our feet to see who could press the servant's button under the oriental rug.

Then my father cut the meat. There was pot roast cooked to a soft gray in onion soup mix and standing rib for occasions. Sometimes there were Swedish meatballs and only rarely my father's favorite, tongue with Spanish rice, which the kids weren't expected to eat. My father led the nightly discussion on current events. He asked my brother questions. My brother could name all the members of the Cabinet except the postmaster general by the time he was nine.

My father went to get the World Almanac from his study. He read from it, to make sure my brother knew all the names, and the spelling. My sister was fishing the last tomato out of the wooden salad bowl, down at her end. She wanted to go upstairs to her room and listen to an Elvis record on the hi-fi and read fashion magazines. She had a dressing table full of lipstick and brushes and combs and colognes. If I behaved right she would let me come in and watch.

I loved to hide in that house. I hid under the grand piano, to watch the argyle socks of my sister's dates. I crouched on the staircase, to watch my parents' parties. I hid behind the couch. Everyone had an activity I wanted to observe.

After dinner, my father sank into the wing chair with a newspaper and smoked L&Ms. A corner of the living room belonged to him, consisting of the wing chair, a table with a chess set on it, and a grand piano across from the table. He sat in that chair and rubbed one hand through his sandy gray hair and leaned his cheek, freckled with white stubble, against a quilted upholstery fabric of green song larks. I can hear the ice clinking in his glass, one of the gold and black glasses they'd gotten as anniversary presents with "Sidney and Leonore" printed on it. He put the glass down by the chess set next to his ashtray and picked up his cigarette and breathed in, a deep sigh of a breath.

My family had made the transition from diaspora Yiddish to American English in a quick generation. You couldn't hear the shadow of an accent, unless my grandmother was around.

Until I heard Risa, a recent Russian immigrant who gives manicures at the Paris Health Club in New York City, I had completely forgotten the sound of my grandmother's accent. I was going there weekly, to the salon, to offset the strains of my untenured teaching job in the French department at Columbia. "Let me see those hands, darling." I closed my eyes and surrendered my hands. Risa laid her hands on mine, deftly scraping away at excess cuticle. It was my grandmother's soft hands, her voice, too. It was Nanny! Her "r" had the same lilt as Risa's, more of a gargle than a roll. There was throat in her voice, too, "acch" sounds and spit. Her "a"s turned into "e"s: "Ellis," not "Alice"; "fess" instead of "face"; "nels" instead of "nails," like Risa's.

My grandmother lived on Fremont Avenue in West Minneapolis in a post-Victorian block of two-family duplexes and brick apartments bordered on one corner by the reform temple, Temple Israel, and on the other by the Red Owl Supermarket. It was a quick walk to pick up sprinkles for sugar cookies or some bridge mix or to go to services. "Don't get in a car with any strangers, don't go with strange boys!" She would give me a lesson when we walked alongside some innocent blonde grocery boy, wheeling the cart to 2410 Fremont Avenue for his twenty-five-cent tip.

Danger was at bay inside her house. Every surface, from the gray nubbly upholstery of the chair next to the window, to the green silk with gold thread covering the couch, to the gray-green oil painting of my glamorous Aunt Helen, spoke of familiarity and comfort. Only books were missing. Three books perched timidly on a built-in bookshelf dividing the dining room from the living room. One of them was a biography of Pola Negri, the star of silent film. My Aunt Stella had worked for her. We knew that Pola Negri lost her stardom when talking films came in. No one in Hollywood liked her accent in the movies, so she retired. I picked up the Pola Negri biography every time I went to my grandmother's and looked for my Aunt Stella in the index. I wished Nanny would get some different books. I suspected she couldn't read or write but I didn't want to ask. She had an acute sense of propriety, for herself and for anyone who was Jewish. "It's a shame for the people" was Nanny's line about any Jewish person who committed a crime, lapsed in behavior, or called attention to themselves.

There were some topics you couldn't bring up around Nanny. The social security form she had to sign remained untouched for months on her coffee table. She had never voted. In her mind an evil force, bigger than the Red Owl, bigger than the Temple, lurking, perhaps, in the Social Security Administration or the Registrar of Voters, was waiting to send her back. Back to Trask, Lithuania, where her mother had hidden her in the closet so the Cossacks wouldn't rape her.

wow.

Looking at a photo of my grandmother when she was my age, thirty-eight, I see that she looked like me. The same lines from her nose to her lips. Low forehead. Full cheeks. A Victorian pompadour, a heavy bodice swathed in gauzy fabric, a high neck. When she was eighty, our family snapshots show her in her pink wallpaper brocade, holding herself primly, her lips pursed disapprovingly.

"Who's that boy? Don't you go with any boys. You don't know what they're going to do with you."

"Nanny, stop it!"

I made fun of my grandmother's warnings. They came out of nowhere. Sometimes I thought she was making a joke. Then I would look at her up close and see the trembling around her mouth, the tightening of her jaw. She was terrified.

My parents thought it was a good idea to have people

other than family members around Nanny. Around out-
siders, she would hide her fears so as not to shame her people. After Nanny moved out of the Fremont Avenue duplex,
I took my friend Valerie Golden to visit Nanny's new apartment on this theory. Valerie was the other Jewish girl in my
class at school. She understood about Nanny. "You can't
come in girls, they're coming for me. Not safe, not safe."
Nanny's vowels were fast and choppy. Her tongue was click-
ing against the roof of her mouth as she talked through the
door. It barely sounded like English anymore. Valerie and I
never even got her to open. Her sociability had stopped
working.

For eight years she languished in the Sholom Home, on
thorazine. The Sholom Home nursing facility, serving the
Jewish community, was located in a no-man's-land between
the Twin Cities of Minneapolis and St. Paul. You had to follow the freeway signs for "The Midway: State Fairgrounds"
to get there. The false promise of those freeway signs annoyed me.

At Sholom I could hear the foreign din as soon as I walked
in the door. Old people sat in groups and spoke Yiddish.
There was a singular quality to the sounds of the Sholom
Home that disturbed me: they were familiar, although I
couldn't understand a word.

Nanny didn't sit with the others. She sat in her room on
her Victorian chair from Fremont Avenue, rocking and
wringing her fleshy hands. A fuse had blown in her head,
making it impossible for her to control which language she
was speaking. The languages from her past—Russian from
the school she had attended in Lithuania, Yiddish from
home, Hebrew from the synagogue—came up like bile. She

had gotten a prayer book as a gift from the Sholom Home administration. She wore it around her neck on a chord. She picked it up and closed her eyes, started in on a prayer, looked up at me, and "recognized" me. "Oh my, I don't know what I'm saying, Ruthie" (Ruthie was my aunt); then she stiffened and went silent. The next words she spoke were in Yiddish. The mode of each language was in place: her Hebrew sounded incantatory, ritualistic; Yiddish was conversational, emotional. The change from one language to another, from ritual to conversation, was all the communication she could produce.

I had never heard my grandmother speak more than a sentence or two in a foreign language until she lost her mind. She had kept those past lives tight inside her, until they came out all jumbled up at the end. I would give anything to have heard her when she was ten or twenty or thirty-five, when her other languages worked. I imagine my Nanny in the czar's school. She's an ace at Russian in my fantasy. Even though it's the language of evil men, she picks it up right away. It protects her from them. I invent a scene: a wooden desk, a smock, Cyrillic letters on slate, pens and inkwells.

Today I am a French teacher. I think about my Nanny, sliding from Hebrew to English to Yiddish. Sliding and pushing away bad memories. Nanny had a surfeit of memories, but there was no connection between one memory and the next. "Il n'y avait pas de suite dans ses idées": "There was no connection between her ideas." Why does that sentence come to me in French, out of the blue? It flies into my head. No other sentence will do. I wonder why I switch like that— why I suddenly need to think in French. It's not like my

13

grandmother's switching, but it feels disturbed, like hers. French, for me, is not just an accomplishment. It's a need. I wonder if I could end up like her?

The Last Summer at Wildhurst Road

Until I was eight, we spent every summer at our lake house on Wildhurst Road, Lake Minnetonka. We stayed there from Memorial Day until Labor Day. It was a square, white stucco, two-story house built by my grandfather Max Kaplan before he lost his money in the Depression. A stone wall along the lakefront had fallen into disrepair but the dock my parents put up got more elaborate every year. By the time I was seven, the dock was grand: you walked out thirty feet or more to a generous square that you could lie on, fish off, or dive off. The important rooms of the house faced the lake. Downstairs there was a square room the whole length of the house on the lake side, where you could watch the sun set. Upstairs there was a sleeping porch with windows on three sides where my parents slept. It was a romantic, peaceful room with a view of Lake Minnetonka through elm trees and a constant warm breeze. In town my parents slept in twin beds but at the lake house they slept together in my grandmother's mahogany bed, looking out at the lake. At the lake we lived in closer quarters than in town. My room was connected to my parents' sleeping porch by a glass door, with a curtain for privacy. There was no hallway separating us. I looked out the windows of my room onto the next-door neighbors' house. I could hear the sound of the lake lapping against the shore coming in through my parents' sleeping porch. Daylight savings meant that dusk didn't come until 9 P.M. I heard too many interesting noises to want to sleep: crickets, waves lapping against the shore, the purr of outboard motors.

A whole different network of friends lived out at the lake: on Grays Bay, Tonka Bay, Wayzata Bay, past the Narrows Bridge. I loved visiting people by boat instead of by car. My sister took me over to her friend Tuppy's, on the Upper Lake. I got to play with Tuppy's little sister Gretchen. Once, when night fell, a bat came into the house through an open window. We couldn't see it but we could hear the swish of the wings. We turned on the light in the living room, and the bat cast its shadow on the walls. It looked like it knew where it was going, swooping under doorways at scientific angles.

Tuppy and Gretchen's parents weren't home. We ran through the house, screaming, as if our screams would make the bat go away. We laughed at the sight of each other running through the house and screaming. We laughed until we cried, tears of exhaustion and pleasure at our game. The bat eventually flew out of the house as expertly as it had come in, then we lay on the couch, the four of us, and breathed long sighs until we were calm again.

In Minnesota you could look up at any night sky in the summer and see the bats swooping around under trees. Bats preferred old barns and garages and attics to living rooms and dining rooms, but occasionally they got trapped and had to feel their way out of a human abode.

I was in my room on Wildhurst Road, listening to night sounds. The overhead light was still on. I looked up at the ceiling and a bat came swooping between me and the light. I got a good look at its face and wings. The wings made a shadow against the wall of my bedroom, bigger than the bat at Tuppy's. I screamed. My parents came running. My father grabbed a tennis racket from my brother's room. He went running through the house swinging that tennis racket. Tennis wasn't his game. He liked golf and fishing. I had never seen my father move so fast. My mother looked worried—about him, not the bat. It took him an hour to get that bat under control. His face was usually a pale sandy color but now it was red and sweaty. I kept the door to my room open so I could watch, even though that meant the bat might come back in. I watched him run down the hall with the tennis racket over his head. He was swearing. Finally he met up with the bat. He smashed it against a wall. I left my room to get a closer look. He was wrapping the bat in newspaper provided by my mother.

"Mom, I want to see the bat."

"Now, why in the world would you even want to see such a thing? Bats carry horrible diseases."

My mother wrapped up the bat; my father flushed it down the toilet.

I thought back many times on the glimpse I'd had of the bat for a split second, swooping across my head. It had a human face. — significance ?

My parents went out on the lake at night, trolling for walleyed pike. I saw them leave, my mother in an oversize plaid shirt and my father wearing khaki pants and a khaki shirt, carrying the fishing gear. His sandy hair and sandy skin and the khaki made him look all one color.

My brother explained trolling: "It's a special way of fishing. You need a quiet boat and a long line. You take your time. You let your line move along the water with the movement of the boat. There are fish you can catch off a dock and fish you can only catch trolling. Daddy knows the places on the lake where the fish like to go."

Fish would like a place with lots of seaweed, willow trees hanging over the water, frogs, flies on the surface. I imagined my parents in a secret cove, way on the other side of the lake, with fish jumping out at them.

I pleaded with my brother: "Please, please wake me up when they get home so I can see what they catch!" I heard the sound of their motor coming toward the dock from my bedroom. By then I was already half asleep, dreaming of bats and fish.

My father taught me how to clean sunfish and crappies. He covered the top of a retaining wall to one side of our house in newspaper and transferred the wet fish from a bucket onto the paper. Sunfish and crappies were little fish, just my size. First you had to take the hook out, which could be hard depending on where it was lodged. You knew the fish was fresh if its eye was clear. If the eye was cloudy, you threw it away. My father cut the head off a clear-eyed fish. He slit the fish open and scooped the guts out of the inside. He pointed out the orange globs inside, which meant that the fish was pregnant. I got so I could tell, just by looking at the curve of their belly, which fish would have eggs inside. He scooped out the orange globs. He scraped the scales off the fish with a scaling knife until it was smooth. I felt what the fish felt like when it first came off the line, when the scales could stick into your hand. I felt how smooth it was by the time he got done with it. He rinsed the scaled fish in the kitchen sink, dried it with a white flour-sack dish towel, dipped it in flour. He took a cast-iron pan and melted butter until the butter was nut brown. Then he fried the fish in the butter. We sat around a round table on the screened-in porch facing Wildhurst Road and ate crisp buttery fish with lemon slices.

My first fishing pole was made of bamboo and it had a red and white bobber to weigh the hook down. I sat on the dock with my father, my feet dangling in the water. I had my bamboo fishing pole; he had a rod and reel. My father was showing me how to cast his rod out on the water and reel it back in right away, feeling for the tug of the small crappie or the pike. Again and again, whether you get anything or not you fling it out there. You can just see the flies up on the surface of the water where it hits, when it's dark. We didn't talk much that evening, it was the perfect quiet time before the crickets get into full voice. I hardly noticed him slipping away, "not feeling great, going into the house for a drink of water," is what he said. I stayed on the dock another hour, fiddling with the fishing pole. I went back in the house through the back door. My brother was sitting on a chair looking out at the lake, pretending to read a book. I said to my brother, "Where are Mom and Dad?" (the last time I said "Mom and Dad" in the present tense).

"They went to the hospital for a checkup."

"Oh."

He was in one of those moods where I wouldn't get any more information out of him, so I went up to bed in my room off the sleeping porch. I didn't believe him, though. Why would they go for a checkup at night?

In the middle of the night, I heard my mother come into my room. She sat on the side of my bed and nudged me instead of going into the sleeping porch. I rubbed my eyes and looked up at her. She looked like a shadow of herself because of the way the moonlight came in through my window. She said, "Your father is dead."

I went downstairs with her. Other grownups were there. They were sitting in the official living room, not the room facing the lake where we usually sat. They were wide awake, even though it was the middle of the night. My mother talked. She told them each remark my father had made that day about how he was feeling. She had discovered a note in his top drawer, among the ties, telling him how to cut down on his cigarettes. He hadn't shown any signs of quitting. He hadn't said a thing about it. She curled up in the chaise lounge by the piano under one of my grandmother's crocheted afghans. They talked a long time, going over the details of his last week, over and over. He shouldn't have moved that pile of wood onto the neighbor's yard. He wasn't in any shape. By the time he got to the hospital he was gone. A massive coronary. There was nothing Reuben could do for him. How awful for Reuben.

When I went back up to sleep I slept soundly. I had this dream: the word "New York" had become "Yew Nork." I was going to Yew Nork, and I was laughing at my joke. There was a red balloon in the dream too. When I woke up again, the sun was coming in through the windows, a perfect June day.

It is awful to learn about death in the middle of the night. Because when you wake up in the morning the sun is out and you are quite sure it couldn't have happened. You have to realize it all over again. That's how it was, for me.

Levine Blue was already at the house when I woke up. She came up to my room to see how I was doing. I told her my dream. "It's gonna be all right, girl," she said, looking at me. "I guess I won't have to wash all these ashtrays anymore." She was holding a cut crystal ashtray the shape of a top hat in one hand, and rubbing the tobacco stain off the bottom with a dish towel.

I could hear the extra voices downstairs. Cars came up the gravel driveway and parked in a circle all around it. The screen door opened and shut. By the time I got downstairs, people were standing up because there weren't enough chairs. People were huddled around my mother, still in her chaise. A neighbor had made some cookies in the shape of the letters S and K, my father's initials, and my sister and brother and I made jokes about the cookies. My neck hurt from looking up at all the people looking down at me.

The next morning, the morning of my father's funeral, was my eighth birthday. I wanted to wear black, but my mother said that I was too young to wear black so I wore my light blue dress with the petticoat. "You don't need a black dress, you're a little girl!" The sun came in through my bedroom window and made the dress look even lighter than it was.

My mother and sister and brother and I drove to the military cemetery in the back of a big black car that wasn't ours. We sat on folding chairs in front of the grave. Everybody else had to stand. My chair squeaked every time I moved. I concentrated on keeping my chair from squeaking and afterwards I made jokes about it. Finally some soldiers folded the flag in the shape of a triangle and gave it to my mother. She wouldn't let them give the ten gun salute because she didn't like guns; she had told us about that before.

We drove home. The wife of my father's law partner whom I barely knew brought a birthday cake to the house after the funeral. It had white frosting, frosting curlicues, my name, and the number "8" in the middle in silver balls. The adults whispered to each other about what to do and then they sang me Happy Birthday. I didn't know what to do, I didn't want the song. I put my head down so I wouldn't have to see any of them singing to me. Even though I wasn't looking, I could feel their smiles on me, fake smiles. I crossed one leg over the other and squirmed. When the singing stopped I opened some presents, a white sweater with shiny beads on it from the wife of my father's partner, and a set of watercolors. The watercolor set was my chance to get away. "Thank you very much may I go out now?"

"Yes dear."

A woman I had never seen before called me "dear."

I went out on the dock again, where my father and I were together before he died. I took my watercolor set with me, a neat white box with the Swiss mountain on the lid. First I tried to paint the lake and the trees across the lake, but I couldn't get it to look right, so I changed the trees into mountains like on the watercolor box. I thought mountains would be easier. The green and the brown paint ran together until the whole thing was a mess. When I crumpled the paper in my hand it was soggy from too much paint.

My father had been gone for three weeks. I was lying in my bed, looking straight up at the ceiling, listening to the noises downstairs. My mother was with house guests who had arrived after the funeral. The door to the sleeping porch was closed. My mother came upstairs, walked through my room, and opened the door between her room and mine. She shut it, hard, a split second later. I could hear her suck her breath in, fast. "Oh my god!"

The light was on in the sleeping porch. I got up, stood next to her, lifted the curtain, pressed my nose against the glass pane. For a minute I couldn't tell what I was seeing. Black darts were zooming in every conceivable bat pattern across the room. There were so many bats, moving so fast, it looked like they were making wind.

"Kids, kids, there are bats everywhere!"

It was hopeless. My father was gone, there was no one to go after the bats with tennis rackets and flush them down the toilet. Besides, even if he had been around, we now had too many bats for one man to kill. It was beyond anything my father could have helped with.

We all slept downstairs that night, my mother, us kids, the house guests. The exterminator who came to the house the next day found bats hanging from the top of my parents' sleeping porch curtains in thick bunches. He used a chemical to kill them. He told us that entire nests of bats must have hatched in the eaves over the sleeping porch. Holes in the window and eaves construction had allowed them in but not out. They were babies, he added. There was really nowhere for them to go after they hatched except the sleeping porch. They couldn't get out into the night sky.

One bat was enterprising enough to escape the chemical attack and make its way from the sleeping porch to the other end of the upstairs hall and into a closet in my brother's room. My brother was spending so much time in his room with the door closed since my father died that I couldn't figure out how the bat had gotten in there, but it had. It jumped out at my brother when he went into his closet to get a pair of shoes.

I tried to be ready to look a bat in the eye that summer, every time I opened a door, or even a drawer. I laid my head on the pillow. I heard crickets, water lapping up on the shore, and the whoosh of bat wings in my head.

After my father died, there were a few more summers on Wildhurst Road; I can't remember them. The eaves on the house were thoroughly repaired to prevent the comings and goings of bats. My mother rented the house for several years, then sold it.

Loss

I walk into my mother's closet. It is full of bright colors and delicate patterns. There is a faint odor of talcum power in the air. Clothes are smashed together; the patterns of a black lace nightgown stand out against a solid blue silk dress. These are the fabrics of a life my mother has with my father when she is not wearing her car coat or her garden smock or her plaid fishing shirt. I recognize the dress from a photograph on my parents' dresser. In the photograph, my mother and father stand on a dance floor, poised for a fox trot. At age fifty, the outlines of my father's face have started to spread; his hair has thinned. He is looking at the camera with a grim smile set on a closed mouth. He must not like dancing. My mother, half a head shorter than he, is wearing the silk dress and a string of pearls that sets off her black hair. Her smile is rushed. She has her eye on someone to the right of the camera; she's waiting for the picture to be taken so she can continue a conversation.

I reach up to touch her clothes. I feel the crinkles of the lace. I run my cheek, which only comes up as high as the skirt, over the rough silk fabric.

I walk into the same closet three years later. It is empty, except for a zipped plastic bag smelling of moth balls. There is not a hanger in sight. I breathe in the ammonia from the moth balls. There is dust on the wood floor. My mother has moved her clothes downstairs to a new bedroom where the den used to be.

My sister is going away to college in two weeks. She and my mother let me come along when they go shopping at Peck and Peck for my sister's college wardrobe. My sister tries on a worsted wool suit in different shades of brown and yellow. I stand behind her in the dressing room; I watch her put on her college outfits; I watch her college face in the mirror. A neighbor has given her a bottle of perfume for a going-away present: "L'air du temps" by Nina Ricci. She even smells different.

My grandmother is at our house for dinner. My mother starts to cry, so quietly I can't tell except for a tear or two that shows on her face. She excuses herself from the table. "Your mother has an infected finger, you know," my grandmother explains. "I know, Nanny." I have seen my mother's hands, formerly soft and smooth to the touch, looking bony, with a gauze dressing and bandage on one finger. I walk into my mother's downstairs bedroom to say good night. She isn't under the covers. She is lying on top of the bedspread, wrapped in an afghan, her head on the pillow, her eyes closed. I don't wake her. I try to sleep in my room on the second floor. "She'll be dead in the morning, when I wake up my mother will be dead and I'll be an orphan." I rehearse my fear.

When I am upstairs, alone, I walk from room to room, looking in all the closets. I play a game to see how many hints of each person remain in the room they vacated. Every room in the house has changed. I've moved into my sister's room. My brother has moved to the two rooms behind the back stair case where I used to sleep. My mother has moved to the den downstairs. The television room has moved to the bedroom upstairs, where my brother's room used to be. I walk into the bathroom that is now all mine and remember the time my sister and her friend locked themselves in there because they didn't want my brother and me bothering them. I walk in my parents' old room and smell the mothballs in the closet. I walk up to the attic and open the trap door where the attic fan vents onto the second floor landing. I look down at the second floor from on high. No one sees me.

I take my trolls, three little plastic monsters with swatches of red hair, and line them up on the windowsill with props. I take Instamatic pictures of them so when the pictures get developed it looks like they are human size and live in the real world.

My mother got rid of my father's clothes so efficiently that I didn't know they were gone until I snooped around upstairs. She didn't get rid of his books, though. Books on Stalin and Hitler and Truman and Roosevelt, all the volumes of the Nuremberg trials still lined his study. My father was a lawyer at the Nuremberg War Crimes trials where they punished Nazi war criminals. He was connected to a world more significant than ours, to important men in suits and uniforms, to good and evil itself.

I asked my mother what happened to people after they died. "Jews do not believe in an afterlife. We believe that people live on through their achievements." That year in school, third grade, I racked up sixty book reports.

My mother kept the flag from my father's funeral on the

top shelf of the closet in her new bedroom downstairs. Every week or so, if no one was looking, I opened the closet door to see if the flag was still there or if she'd given it away.

My mother gave each of us a copy of the letters my father had written to her from Nuremberg. She had them typed onto onionskin paper and bound in a green folder. There was a picture of my father in the folder, wearing a uniform. There was an engraving of the city of Nuremberg before it was bombed. There was a folding chart of the Nazi chain of command. In the letters, my father told what he was eating and drinking, what plays he was seeing, what arrangements he was making to come home to my mother. My mother was in Chevy Chase with their first child, my sister. My father wanted to know how the baby's formula was working, were her bowel movements normal, was she sleeping through the night. Preparations for the most important trial since the trial of Jesus Christ were a snafu. He would talk to Robert Jackson as soon as the war of aggression section was written up. He wanted to come home to his daughter.

I have a cold-war imagination. My image for forgetting and repressing is an iron curtain coming down in front of my face, a curtain like the curtain at a play, only hardened, rippled in place in such a way that it looks at a distance like regular cloth.

The first business letter that was ever addressed to me came from Radio Free Europe, a radio station broadcasting for the Free World from Behind the Iron Curtain. The letter came with its own return envelope. I sent back a dollar and got a thank-you note from Bradford Simpson, Ford Simpson's father and chairman of RFE's Minnesota branch. Radio Free Europe was a bunch of right-wing Republicans, I knew what that meant when I was six, but it didn't stop me from mailing in my dollar. It was my right, like the right to get the toy out of the Cracker Jacks. I grew up in an age of clipping and saving cereal box tops, Bazooka Joe cartoons, and the S&H green stamps that my grandmother let me lick into her premium books.

From the vestibule, where I read my letter from Radio Free Europe, I could walk down the hall between the front staircase and the living room (where the record player was), and straight to my father's library. The room was dark: there was a huge mahogany desk, built into a wall, surrounded by shelves. There was a gigantic leather lounge chair that vibrated if you pushed a button ("the contour chair," we called it, by its brand name) and a steam-filled radiator, hissing slightly, where the magazines sat on a trellised radiator cover. On the desk was a blotter in a frame of leather, ink doodles on the blotter, real cartridge-pen ink. The black Underwood adding machine occupied the space to the right of the blotter.

My mother sat at my father's mahogany desk and wrote bills. She calculated her income on the black Underwood adding machine. I was allowed to sit at the desk, too, and do my homework. *The World Book Encyclopedia* was on the first left shelf, so I could look up facts.

I made a thorough search of my father's desk. I opened every drawer and every box in every drawer. Yellow legal pads covered with his writing were stacked to the top of the left file drawer. In the right bottom drawer I found gray cardboard boxes. There were black and white photographs of dead bodies in them. In several photographs hundreds of bony corpses were piled on top of one another in giant heaps. I had never seen a dead body, not even in a photograph. When Mrs. Nelson, my first-grade teacher, died in the fall of second grade, I didn't have to go to the funeral because there was an open coffin. "It isn't right for a little girl to have to look at her teacher's corpse." Here, multiplied by thousands, was what I wasn't supposed to see. This was what death looked like.

Not every body in the photographs was dead. People were standing up, but they didn't look human. Their bones stuck out too much. You could see the sockets where one bone connected to the next. Some were naked, some wore striped pajamas that fell off their bones. One man tried to smile. His face was more frightening than the expressionless faces—he was reaching for life, but it was too late. There were photographs of human hair and teeth and jewelry arranged in neat piles, as though they were being exhibited in a museum. "U.S. Army" and a series of numbers was stamped on the back of each photograph.

My mother told me that the photographs were taken by Mr. Newman. He was a photographer for the Army when they liberated the concentration camps at the end of the war. His photographs were evidence at Nuremberg for what the Nazis did. He had returned to Minneapolis after the war, where he opened a photographic portrait studio.

I took the photos to class to show the other third-graders what had happened in the camps. My mother had gone through the photos and removed the ones she thought were too upsetting, but I wanted to take all of them, especially the upsetting ones, where you could see the death right close up, the way the flesh hung off the skeleton, the hip bones that looked like shelves. I believed in facts. I believed that my friends had no right to live without knowing about these pictures, how could they look so pleased when they were so ignorant. None of them knew what I knew, I thought. I hated them for it.

I explained to them about the camps, Hitler, how many Jews had died. To shock them. They had to know! I had to tell them. Or was it just that I missed my father. I was trying to do what he would do, be like him.

My mother got the idea that she would take us to live in the South of France. She had a specific city in mind, Montpellier. What was my image of France, then? I imagined a house where we would be together near the water, the way we were together in the summers on Wildhurst Road. My mother said there would be palm trees and warmth in Montpellier. "I need a change," she said, "I need warmth."

From her sleepy, afghan-wrapped cocoon, she went into high gear, arranging a passport photograph for herself, me, my brother. She hired Mr. Newman, the concentration camp photographer, to take our passport photos. For no extra charge, he offered to take a group portrait of the three of us.

Oh sunny France, I can see myself there underneath a palm tree. I will be a French girl, like Madeline in the Madeline books who lives in an orphanage with other girls and walks in a straight line and gets a visit from Miss Clavel when she goes into the hospital with appendicitis. My brother thinks France is a dumb idea. Why should he leave his friends to go to some place where he knows no one, where he's never been, where he's never wanted to go. Besides, he takes German.

In Mr. Newman's group portrait, my mother is looking far into the distance. The cheeks that were round and glowing in the portrait of her dancing with my father are sunken in.

My brother looks carved in stone; his jaw is clenched. I am the only one in the picture with my mouth open (I have an overbite and can't close it). I am the only one who is smiling. I want to go to France.

President Kennedy was assassinated in 1963, a year and a half after my father died on Wildhurst Road. My mother had abandoned her France plan by then. The opening of my brother's school play, *A Thurber Carnival*, fell the night of the assassination. My mother and I sat in the audience, waiting for the word that the show had been canceled. A student came on stage and said JFK would have wanted the show to go on.

My mother and my brother and I sat close together in the TV room upstairs and watched the funeral of JFK. There was a flag folded in a triangle, just like at my father's funeral. A soldier handed the flag to Jacqueline Kennedy just as a soldier had handed it to my mother. The newscasters commented on the world leaders as they walked down Pennsylvania Avenue. De Gaulle, the president of France, floated over the rest. He wore a hat that reminded me of Abraham Lincoln's stovepipe hat, only shorter. Instead of a band all around it there was a visor in front that stuck out in line with his enormous nose. The newsmen commented on the special relationship of de Gaulle and Jacqueline Kennedy, who was able to speak to him in fluent French. I learned from Kennedy's funeral that Washington was designed on the model of Paris. The Champs Elysées was a grand boulevard that ran between the Arc de Triomphe and the Place de la Concorde; Pennsylvania Avenue ran between the White House and Capitol Hill. The newscaster told how de Gaulle had marched down the Champs Elysées after the liberation of France: "How familiar this funeral procession must feel to the French leader; yet how different in mood."

Thursday night in our house. My brother walks in through the back door. It's snowing in November. His white and brown Blake School football "away game" uniform is black with mud. "We lost. I'm not hungry." He disappears up the back stairs. My mother and I eat dinner together at the yellow linoleum kitchen table. She has gone back to work for the Hennepin County Department of Welfare, where she had worked during the Depression before she got married. Work has revived her. "You wouldn't believe the language they use!" Her clients say "horse's ass" and "motherfucker" and "fuck you." She talks in horror about the way they talk back to her. I can tell she likes their swearing. Maybe, secretly, she would like to swear, too.

What am I doing? In third grade I am racing to get the most book reports. I read every orange biography in the series of Famous Lives. I read some of them in ten minutes, to rack up another report. In fourth grade, the year Kennedy dies, I am playing "heads or tails" in the cloak room with Mary S, the tallest girl in our class, who has a coin she stole from her father with a woman's breasts on one side and her bottom on the other. In fifth grade I am in Mrs. Larkin's homeroom. She rewards us for work well done with a red witch sticker. In Mrs. Larkin's history class we try to understand the passage of time. We wind a string around and around the playground. The string represents the number of years since Dr. Leakey's Man roamed the earth. In Mrs. Larkin's class I watch Walter Cronkite interview Socrates before he takes the hemlock in "You Were There at the Death of Socrates."

33

In fifth grade I am taking my first French class with Mrs. Holmgren, watching the hair on her legs through her nylon stockings, registering her foreignness. As ringleader of our French class, I organize us to put alarm clocks in our desks, each one set to go off at the exact same moment in the middle of Madame Holmgren's French lesson.

"Ah mon Dieu. Qu'est-ce qui se passe? Mais quel est ce bruit?"

I love to hear Madame Holmgren get upset, in French.

Leaving

My mother and I drove to Wayzata, Minnesota, to find me a dress at the Mother Daughter Shop. They sold mother clothes and daughter clothes on adjoining racks. The daughter clothes didn't fit me, "too tight in the bust," my mother kept saying. In the mother clothes I looked ridiculous—a child imitating an old lady.

The girls in my school wore Lanz dresses to dancing school. The dresses were tight in the rib cage and waist. They fanned out into flouncing skirts. I could not zip a Lanz dress around my rib cage, even if I took three sizes too big.

"It's so hard to find you anything to wear! We'll just have to try again."

"I can't help it! It's not my fault!"

"I didn't say it was your fault, dear."

We drove home back home in silence. As soon as my mother unlocked the door to the house, I ran up the back stairs and slammed the door of my room. A voice in my head was saying, "You're in a bad mood because you're an adolescent." I had been reading *Youth: The Years from Ten to Sixteen*, by Arnold Gesell, kept on the shelf in the TV room. It showed everything that happened to an adolescent: there was a picture of the shape changes in the adolescent body and a description of the adolescent mood which included unexpected bursts of temper. It didn't help my mood to know I was an adolescent; knowing I was one seemed like part of something awful that was happening to me. I kept seeing myself from outside myself, as though I were always looking at myself in a book. But I couldn't change the book.

I called Connie, my closest friend living within walking distance of my house.

"Help, I think I got my period."

"How do you know?"

"It's not like real blood. It's brown."

"Gross!"

"I don't have any Kotex."

"So ask your mother."

"Forget it."

"What do you mean, forget it."

"Just forget it. I'm not telling."

"Alice!"

"She bugs me. She'll make a big deal out of it."

"So go to the drugstore."

"No, I feel too queer."

"All right, all right, I've got an emergency kit with six Kotex and a belt. My mother gave it to me when I turned eleven. You can have it. But you better figure something out for later. This is going to happen to you again, you know.".

I studied the construction of the Kotex. I could simulate it with a few layers of toilet paper. This method worked for a year, but it destroyed my underwear. I hid them, pair by pair, in a corner of the closet. Levine Blue found them when she was cleaning up:

"For goodness sakes, why didn't you tell me you got your period."

My mother called me downstairs to her room in back of the house. She was lying on the bed in her characteristic pose, wrapped in the beige afghan.

"It's no big deal."

"Imagine my shock when Levine told me. Really, Alice, what is the matter with you?"

"Nothing. It's no big deal. Just forget it."

I didn't know what age I was. Chronologically I was twelve, but I corresponded more closely to the Gesell chapter on age sixteen. I thought I might be even older inside and was forced to live as a child. I thought that my father dying meant that I couldn't be a child even if I wanted to, that I had to toughen up. I thought that getting my period early was a test, to see if I could take care of myself. My body had gone on ahead of me to see if I could catch up.

At fourteen I had Mrs. Hill, a legendary teacher, for ninth-grade physics. I could see the gleam in the eyes of my classmates as Mrs. Hill engaged us in an experiment using the remarkable powers of fulcrums. I looked around, saw how excited they were, and laid my head on my desk. In my head there was a story competing with the story of the fulcrum; it involved a man in a suit coming to rescue me from the schoolroom, taking me to the bank of a river, lowering me onto grass, covering my face with kisses, professing desperate love. I could make the story shorter or longer depending on how much time I had. All I had to do was put my head down on the desk, cover my face with my arms to block out the light, and start the picture going in my head.

Mrs. Hill was sick. Miss Gray, the Headmistress, substituted in physics class. Miss Gray's favorite activity was standing in the hall with her hands folded over her stomach, watching us march into Chapel. The thought crossed my mind that it wasn't a good idea to put my head on the desk in front of Miss Gray, but I didn't have that much control over the situation. Once the story started rolling in my head, I couldn't keep upright. Miss Gray called my house that night and asked my mother, "Is she anemic? Is she often like that with her head in her hands, sleeping all day long, she who used to like facts and had more book reports than anyone?"

My mother consulted with Miss Gray and came up with a Solution. What did I think about going to Switzerland for a year? It would be good for me to get away. It was too limiting here. "I would have taken you kids to Europe after Daddy died, you know, but your brother didn't want to go: he didn't want to leave his friends. You're more adventurous than your brother—you go." That made me want to go, to be more adventurous than my brother.

My mother remembered a trip she had taken to Europe, with her sisters, in 1938: they had to come home, finally, because the Nazis had invaded Czechoslovakia. They had seen Paris and Biarritz and Rome. They even met a Count in Italy. My mother was ambitious for me to go to Switzerland, in her place.

"Europe is just what the doctor ordered."

"Think how good it will be for your French."

"You're more mature than other girls your age."

Mrs. Landanius, wife of the Swedish consul general, mother of my classmate Hedwig, had already investigated every boarding school in Switzerland with the design of sending Hedwig, whose prospects in the world were international. Some of the schools had been too flimsy academically, some were too military, some were too American. Mrs. Landanius recommended a school with discipline and good French instruction: Le Collège du Léman. I sent in my application.

Ninth grade was traditionally the year when the richest girls in my school made their move to boarding schools on the East Coast. My friend Louise was going to the Concord Academy in Concord, Massachusetts. She told me that she wanted to go to a place where the other kids were as rich as she was, so she wouldn't feel strange. The girls at Northrop Collegiate were rich, but apparently there were girls on the East Coast who made our classmates look shabby and provincial. "It isn't about having money, it's about culture," Louise explained to me as she served us Fresca-on-ice in heavy Steuben glasses. The Fresca at her house tasted drier than at mine.

The summer before I went away to Switzerland, Louise took me to a Woodhill Country Club dance where I met Ted.

Ted wore a pink Brooks Brothers shirt to show off his tan. In the winter he played hockey. He was thick, but not too thick, big enough to make me feel small when we danced. Knowing there were no Jewish members at Woodhill gave me a thrill whenever I was there. The night I met Ted I felt like a spy, charming him undercover.

In August Ted and I spent a whole night in bed together in the maid's room of Louise's house. We did everything two people could do in bed without actually taking our clothes off. Neither of us was old enough to drive a car. Ted's father brought him into town to see me one last time, the day before I left for Switzerland.

Ted was a Wayzata boy; he didn't know the city. I took him on a walk around the lakes near my house. We wandered into Lakewood Cemetery, knowing we could be alone there to curl up on the grass. We went looking for our spot.

Ted put his arm around me as we walked and teased me about going away. He told me he was afraid I wouldn't want to talk to him when I got back.

"My sister changed completely at Madeira. You're going even farther. You'll be so European, you won't even remember old Ted."

I loved his slow way of talking. I loved imagining coming home, suave and seductive, before I even left. I wanted to lie down with him. We walked and walked through the cemetery looking for the best place to say goodbye for an entire year. Ted pointed to a grave marked "Alice": "Alice Bergstrand 1893–1920."

"She wasn't very old when she died."

We lay on the grass next to the grave and kissed. Ted squirmed, he was embarrassed about being in the cemetery. This was getting kind of weird. What if we got caught? I wasn't embarrassed. I kissed Ted with total abandon, knowing I wouldn't see him the next day. No one at my new school would know anything about me, including this. I could tell them whatever I wanted. I rolled myself over, with Ted above me, until I felt the marble of the Alice grave under my back. It was a perfect feeling: cool marble below; warm thick Ted above. When I was a kid I had always imagined with my friends that if we dug in the soil far enough we'd come out in China. Now I imagined the grave would open up for me, I'd fall through a trap door and come out on the other side of the world, in Switzerland. I'd be a new person. I wouldn't recognize Ted anymore. I wouldn't even understand his language.

It was a hot, humid August day. The marble on Alice Bergstrand's grave was refreshing. Ted's kisses came faster. I got dizzy from the cold of the marble, the warmth from Ted's mouth; I felt myself cutting, cutting through time and space, slipping through a trap door into another world. I rolled over one last time to get hold of myself. Ted was starting to squash me. With my hands on the marble, I propped myself up over him. His eyes were closed so I didn't need to look at him. I looked around me. The hill was covered with tombstones, the grass was as dark and lush as it ever gets in Minnesota—the heat was making it shimmer in the distance. I could see the lake with a few sailboats on it, across Lake Calhoun Boulevard. It wasn't my home anymore. It was a landscape.

Part Two: *Getting It*

Boarding School in Switzerland

"Bonjour. Je m'appelle Alice Kaplan. Je suis à l'aéroport. Pouvez-vous venir me prendre?" I called the school to pick me up and stood in the Geneva airport, listening to French, waiting.

The driver came in a Mercedes van. He looked like a soccer player. He said to me in French: "Don't try to speak to me in English because I don't understand." He was testing me. He said, "Where are your bags?" The word came up from my throat. "Là-bas," I said, pointing.

My school was in a village in the suburbs of Geneva that was famous because an American adventure story writer and a Scottish racing car driver lived there. The headmaster was Egyptian, and the owner was a wealthy Swiss businessman with another boarding school in the mountains. The racing car driver had insisted that the township invest in safety devices on either side of the road so cars wouldn't drive off the side. My driver entertained me with this story on the way to school. The racing car driver still liked to drive through the town like hell on wheels but the safety devices protected him. I understood from this that the town had a kind of safety net. I couldn't get in trouble there.

That first afternoon I met my roommate, Stephanie, who had just arrived from Germany. She would live in the dorm in order to learn French, because her father had relocated to Geneva for tax purposes, and the whole family had to learn to get along in the new language. I drove with Stephanie and her brother and their father in another padded leather Mercedes, a sedan, down to Lake Léman, and we drank a sweet green mint drink. None of us spoke much, we didn't have the words yet. But we went on the lake in paddle boats and Stephanie taught me: "Das ist eine kleine Möwe" ("that is a small seagull"). It was a good beginning. Then we drove back to the school. I told Stephanie in French, "tell your father thank you," and Stephanie told me he wasn't her father, he was their driver.

I had two other roommates, Chris and Laura. Chris's father was an American NATO general. Her mother was French and beautiful. They were stationed at a base in Stuttgart and sent large boxes of Bazooka bubble gum from the PX. Chris strutted around the room; she walked with a swayback and her stomach stuck out—she admired her own stomach, patting it as if it was a stuffed animal. She watched me undress. She challenged us to see who could stick their stomach out the farthest. She dared me to put on my sweater without a bra. At night she massaged her face with cold creams wearing a special lace camisole her mother had given her for her nightly toilette. When Chris saw I was getting thin she brought me presents of white chocolate. She laid the white chocolate bars on my bed hoping I'd fatten up, but I gave them back. I hated her soft cunning voice, the voice she used when she gave me presents, and her perfect accent in three languages she couldn't spell in—French, German, and English. Laura was the other

American—a Cuban, from Grosse Pointe, Michigan, sent to Switzerland by her parents because she w⁒ too "wild." She spoke English with a tough thud.

At night we would lie in our bunks under our yellow and white striped "poof" coverlets, and Chris would whisper to Stephanie in her southern German accent—lots of soft "ch" sounds—so that Laura and I couldn't understand. "What the hell are they talking about?" Laura said. At first there was just the swish of soft "ch"s. Then I started discriminating the vowels from the consonants. The same sounds repeated themselves again and again—those were words—and then I could hear the difference between the verbs and the nouns. I heard the articles that went with the nouns, and then I heard where the nouns and the verbs went in sentences. One night I heard Chris say the words "Jude," "Jude": I don't know where I recognized the words from—maybe papers in my father's desk—but I knew those words meant "Jewish" and that Chris was telling Stephanie I was Jewish. "Don't think you can talk about me behind my back right in front of me, Chris, just because you're talking German—I understand, you know." I *could* understand. Just by lying there with my ear and listening, I could understand languages. And because I could understand languages, she couldn't get me.

Every night I lay in bed on my bottom bunk and listened, sometimes I felt like I had radar or an antenna sticking out of my ear that could capture any sound. Our rooms had loudspeakers in them, and every morning we were awakened by the Swiss news, in French, and then the monitrice, Laurella, got on the mike to tell us "five minutes to study hall." Every morning those sounds woke me up. I understood more and more until I could anticipate the morning greeting of the

languages open up so many doorways

47

Swiss news, and lip synch, word for word, the standard formulae. I got used to looking at people from a distance, trying to figure out what language they were speaking by the merest shadow of sound floating my way or by their gestures. I always had five or six new words on a personal in-progress list. Each time I heard one of the words on my list, I would notice the context and try to figure out the meaning. When I thought I had the meaning I would wait for the word to come up again, so I could check if my meaning was still right. Finally, I'd try the word out to see if a strange look came over the face of the person I was talking to. If it didn't, I knew I was home free. I had a new word.

I started thinking of my ear as something strong, and precious. I couldn't stand Chris's strutting and whispering, so when the girl in the room next door moved upstairs I moved into her old room, where everyone, a Palestinian and an Italian and a French girl, spoke French all the time. I had the bottom bunk again, and I lay under the yellow and white striped covers and listened.

My ear was getting stronger and stronger.

I kept the Collège du Léman yearbook, which lists the school's official goals: "education based on the solidarity of nations, instilling the love of peace, truth and respect for all races and nationalities, to combine in its teaching the best of the Anglo-American and French cultures, and be international in the human relations it would seek to foster within its walls." There were two of everything at the school: a tenth grade and then the French equivalent, "Seconde"; a senior year preparing for the SAT's or the O levels and a "Classe Terminale" preparing for the French baccalaureate; House prefects if they spoke English or moniteurs and monitrices if they spoke French. The director's greatest achievement was also inscribed in the yearbook: "to assume a heavy and thankless burden of establishing and maintaining standards of behavior which in our tormented age are increasingly called in question without any intellectually credible or morally viable alternative being offered to replace them." It was one year after the French student revolts of 1968. The school was on alert.

Wealthy parents from all over the world who didn't know what to do with their children sent them to the school. The American oil executives in Libya and Saudi Arabia sent them here. The South Vietnamese general. The Shah's cousin.

There was an Iraqi boy named Karmen who liked to buy pastries for everyone. The baker arrived at the school midmorning in his Deux Chevaux, one of those stripped-down economy Citroëns that opened from the back. Karmen was all sad eyes and wallet, serving up beignets and pains au chocolat to the rest of us. A few years after I left the school I tried to look him up at the home address he had given me in Nice. It was an office. A lot of people at the school didn't have home addresses in the usual sense, because they were in exile. Some people had four or five addresses, depending on the season; they were likely to spend half the year in a big hotel. There was Colette, French and Polynesian, whose mother was a movie star with an apartment in Paris and a suite at the Carleton in Cannes and a chalet in Montana, Switzerland, where the school went to ski. Colette and I walked through the snow to her chalet on a February evening after sunset. A caretaker opened the front door when we started up the steps. She said hello to him, a stranger in the dark in front of a house she only occupied a month out of every year or two. He barely recognized her. I don't know what she expected—cocoa, or high tea, or warmth. She got nothing from him. Colette and I didn't say a word on the way back to the school hotel. I was thinking about our house on Lake Minnetonka. Strangers were living in it now. I peered at Colette through the darkness, trying to imagine what her mother looked like in her starring role in *Beauty and the Beast*. I wondered if Colette was adopted.

In our dorm in Geneva a Palestinian girl, bloated and acned, sat in the bathtub at the end of the hall crying, her friend washing her hair because she didn't know how to wash her own hair. The soap was in her hair and the water was running down her shoulders. Her father beat her. There was another immensely wealthy girl in our dorm who stole compulsively. We were fascinated by her desire to steal. We understood stealing—wanting precious objects, wanting attention.

The school encouraged my belief that I had come through my childhood and that adolescence, too, was behind me. I took up smoking in the smoking room. I drank coffee at breakfast. I studied five hours a day. I listened to the stories of the girls in my dorm, which always seemed grander and more important to me than stories at home because they involved embassies, revolutions, transatlantic divorces.

I watched the other girls closely. Girls with thick manes of hair, the most beautiful girls I had ever seen, French-speaking Lebanese girls. The French-speaking students wore tight wool pullovers, with white shirt cuffs folded over the sweater in a way that made you lust over their wrists, and gold bracelets in rows on their wrists, real gold, from the souks of Arabia. The American girls who had grown up in Saudi Arabia looked like they had walked out of a 1950s Sears catalogue; in Saudi Arabia they lived in their own imaginary American world, unchangeable barbecues and picnics and softball tournaments.

Pam was my best friend. She had grown up in Libya in an oil company community; her parents had separated and she was much too old for her age. She said "hon" and "babe" all the time, like a waitress. She wore dresses of gauze and lace and puffed sleeves, with hems six inches above her knees. She had boyfriends in Libya, older men in their twenties, who told her it was good for her to masturbate. She wore bikinis and gold hoop earrings and bracelets and six or seven rings from the Tripoli gold market. She gave me one. I helped her keep her grades up, showed her how to make her botany drawings. She wanted me to help her be serious. She told me stories about sex and drugs and boyfriends and parties. I was her encyclopedia; she was my dirty magazine. We walked across the marble floor through the salon where Mlle Laurella sat, on our way to smoke a cigarette, and Laurella would say, "oh my dears you are so *mince*," and we would feel smooth and slinky and beautiful.

There was a girl in the dorm named Jean who looked like me. She was serious and studious and did well in the school. We invented a story that we were sisters, and told variations to each other. In the yearbook she wrote: "Dearest sister Alice, Remember that it was your mother who married my father, then divorced him then married your father who died and then remarried my father—what a flighty and fickle woman, wherever she may be!" We loved reinventing our families, exercising our own control over death and divorce. I made up variants on that story to help me get to sleep.

I look back at my handwriting from that year, in an assignment notebook that never got thrown out. It is small and round and perfect, no variation from letter to letter. Mostly what I have on record are conjugations. In basement study hall before breakfast I copied verb conjugations like a monk. I had a French grammar book, *Bled's Spelling*, and I did extra exercises for the exceptions to the rules. I did this work the way someone would run a marathon, waiting to hit the wall at twenty miles, feeling the pain of the wall and running through it. I liked to work before breakfast. I thought I memorized better when my head was light.

I wanted life to be the same every day, and mostly it was. We sat in the living room for mail call and listened for our names to be read, in French, which was how I first heard my name pronounced French style with the accent on the second syllable, ah-LEASE. We had our first study hall before breakfast, our second before dinner, then we walked across a lawn to the dining hall in the old building where the boys lived.

Pam and I went on a diet together, the "grand régime." We took the spongy inside out of the bread and ate the crust. At breakfast we got to put a spoon of jam on the crust. We wrote down what we ate every day; I used the same notebook for food and conjugations. Wednesday. Breakfast: two crusts and coffee. And so on. I wrote "Force de volonté" (force of will) across my notebook, the way other girls wrote "Susie loves Ralph." There was chocolate in every store, on every corner, chocolate bars with colored wrappers showing roses, bottles of milk, nuts in rows of six, three rows deep. For each bar of chocolate I didn't eat I learned a verb.

I grew thinner and thinner. I ate French. *better*

I had come from a house where the patterns had broken down and the death that had broken them was not understood. Now I loved the loudspeaker and the study hall and the marble floor because they made me feel hard and controlled and patterned; the harder I felt the more I felt the sorrowful world behind me grow dim and fake and powerless. In my stomach was an almost constant moaning, as though I were hollowed out inside. Before I got up in the morning I ran my hand over my hip bone, to feel my outlines.

I went into the village in search of French. I went to the train station. I bought tickets to Geneva, "aller et retour à Genève"—that is what you had to say to get a round trip ticket. I loved to let it roll off my tongue, "alleretretour" in one drum roll, "to go and return." I bought tickets just to say it. Most of what I did, in town, I did in order to speak. Complicated conversations at the Tabac, the newsstand, the grocery.

I was the only American who knew French who hadn't grown up in a French-speaking country. I was put in the advanced French class. I was seated on the far right of the room up in front, while all the people who lived in French-speaking countries were in a row down the left side of the classroom. Eric, who was sophisticated and kind of a roué with a long thin neck, was there, and Chris, pouting and playing with her colored pencils in the plastic case. She spent all her time zipping that pencil case back and forth. When called on, they spoke French effortlessly, but begrudgingly—"if you insist, if you insist . . ." I could practically hear it under their breath as they tossed off a sentence. They were bored, the students on the left-hand row, how could they be bored? Frichot, the teacher, calls on me. I feel as if I'm on a stage, the lights go down and the desks disappear. The spot is on me. I'm poised as I speak my lines from the play we're reading. I speak my lines with muscles quavering. I come up again and again on that "r," the sound "r" in French, which is one of the hardest sounds for an American to make.

In September my "r" is clunky, the one I've brought with me from Minnesota. It is like cement overshoes, like wearing wooden clogs in a cathedral. It is like any number of large objects in the world—all of them heavy, all of them out of place, all of them obstacles. *Je le heurte*—I come up against it like a wall.

I didn't realize that my "r" and my vowels were connected. It all went together. By concentrating too much on the "r" I was making it worse because in French vowels are primary and consonants follow from correct vowels. The first priority is for The Mouth to be in the right position to make the vowel sounds: lip muscles forward and tighter than in English, the mouth poised and round. Americans speaking French tend to chomp down hard on their consonants and swallow their vowels all together.

So that feeling of coming onto the "r" like a wall was part of feeling the essence of my American speech patterns in French, feeling them as foreign and awkward. I didn't know at the time how important it was to feel that American "r" like a big lump in my throat and to be dissatisfied about it. Feeling the lump was the first step, the prerequisite to getting rid of it.

It happened over months but it felt like it happened in

one class. I opened my mouth and I opened up; it slid out, smooth and plush, a French "r." It was the sound my cat makes when she wants to go out: between a purr and a meouw, a gurgling deep in the throat. It wasn't loud, it didn't interrupt the other sounds. It was smooth, and suave. It felt—relaxed. It felt normal! I had it. With this "r" I could speak French, I wouldn't be screaming my Americanness every time I spoke. "R" was my passport.

I looked up at my teacher, M. Hervé Frichot, former colonial school teacher from Madagascar. He had a goatee and glasses with thick black frames. He was a skeptic but he was looking at me now with deep respect. He hadn't thought I could do it. He said, "You've done it." He added: "Vowels next." But that was minor. I wasn't worried about the vowels because I knew that since I had gotten the "r," I had already started opening up my vowels. I could perfect them with the same method I had used for the "r": First feeling them wrong, like an impediment, feeling them again and again in their wrongness and then, one day, opening up and letting the right sound come. Relaxing. The "r" was the biggest hurdle; my system was now in place.

I looked over at the students on the left-hand row; suddenly they seemed less menacing. Chris had a meek nervous look on her face. Eric's hair was greasy and he was scratching a red spot on his neck. I saw them, because I was one of them now. — language connects you

That was what woke me up: absorbing a new reality, repeating it, describing it, appreciating it. I felt a pull toward learning I hadn't felt since fifth grade: quiet mastery of a subject. Knowing I knew the material, that I had it down. Knowing how to find out more. Inventing methods for listening and making them habits. Feeling a kind of tickle in my ear at the pleasure of understanding. Then the pleasure of writing down what I had heard and getting every detail, every accent mark right.

The French have a verb for the kind of work I did at the Swiss school: *bosser*, which comes from a word meaning "hunched" and means hunkering down to work, bending down over some precious matter and observing it.

I had found my ability to concentrate. I had woken up from the sleep I had lapsed into on my ninth-grade desk.

The school's idea of learning was essentially French—the old Third Republic idea that knowledge is a concrete body that can be demonstrated and mastered. Memorization, copying, repeating, taking words down in dictation: these practices all come from French schools and they are the practices I excelled in. Don't be original, learn from a ready-made reality ready-to-hand. In French schools for many years, children learned to draw in a class exercise called the *leçon de choses* (lesson of things). They drew objects from either the natural or manufactured world and they labeled them.

My whole year was a *leçon de choses*. There was the world out there, the world of Switzerland and French language, and I drew its contours and labeled it.

In February, the whole school moved up to a ski town in the mountains called Montana (by now I was pronouncing it MohntaNAH, not MonTANa). We skied everyday. It was cold and sunny as we rode the chair lift. We saw crosses where people had died in avalanches, making us feel like brave adventurers. At the end of the ski term, we had a slalom race, one section of the tenth grade against another. I knocked over one flag, but my time was good. The gym teacher took a picture of me coming down the course, with the big number on my parka. I studied the picture and saw the angle of my skis, a perfect hockey-stop angle, sending up snow spray. At home I was the worst in sports; here, miraculously, I was good. It felt like my life had been given to me to start over.

French had saved me. *Affect of Language French = Strength*

When spring came we read *The Great Gatsby* in English class. At the end of the novel, after Gatsby is murdered in his swimming pool, the man telling Gatsby's story talks about the Midwest. He is trying to understand Gatsby, who is from the Midwest. We, in class, were trying to understand Gatsby. I was suspicious of my English teacher, Mrs. Blackburne, because she was always giving us composition topics like "My family doesn't understand me" or "a five-page autobiography"; I thought she was at it again, using Gatsby. I thought she wanted us to identify with Gatsby—Gatsby who, as a youth, kept a self-improvement notebook, Gatsby who reinvented himself as a man of the world.

The man telling Gatsby's story remembered how he felt riding the train back to Minnesota from the East during his own boarding-school holidays. There was a whole page about the train, right near the end of the novel. It had less to do with Gatsby than with this man telling the story, who with the death of Gatsby became suddenly very old, and saw the corruption of his world, and saw how far he had come with all his midwestern hopes, only to be disillusioned. I felt like a forty-year-old man reading the story, a tired New York bond salesman with the best part of my life over. The page about the train and the swollen towns beyond the Ohio made my eyes sting. I couldn't explain it in my paper—it seemed unfair to me that a book could make me feel so much pain and loss, the sharp pain of Gatsby's loneliness and ambition, the dull pain of the storyteller. I identified with Gatsby, who was so self-made that no one could say how he had gotten rich, and so alone in the world that only two people came to his funeral. I identified with Gatsby because I had spent the whole year inventing a myth about my own rebirth and isolation. I couldn't say the obvious about my own life: I was afraid to go home, I was afraid of living alone in the big house with my mother who was sick and unhappy, I was dreading the charade of happiness. I had learned a whole new language at boarding school but it was a language for covering pain, not expressing it. I could feel things about Gatsby and his loneliness that I couldn't feel about myself. I felt sorry for him and protective.

I was sitting at a table in the school's new wing when I came to the end of *The Great Gatsby*. It was afternoon, and the sun was coming in through an especially large window that looked out toward the mountains. I looked up toward the window and let the sun shine right in my eyes. The sunshine made me realize I was crying. I put the book on the table, spine down, to wipe my tears away.

Spring Break

In the spring my mother came to Geneva where I hid her away in a lousy little hotel in Versoix before we took the train together to Paris to meet the Vanderveers for vacation. My high-school French teacher, Mrs. Vanderveer, had organized the trip. Her daughter, Priscilla, who was my age, came, and so did her son, Johnny, a teenager who was mentally retarded at the fourth-grade reading level.

We stayed in one of those hotels in the Latin Quarter that looks tiny from the outside, although when you go in, the staircase goes up forever, the top-floor rooms have sloped ceilings, and the windows look out onto a hundred roofs on which you can see the cats prowling.

When my mother and I finished climbing all the stairs to our little room, there was a bouquet of flowers waiting for us: Mr. D had sent them.

Mr. D was a francophile in the grand manner. He owned a big department store in Minneapolis, and he collected art. He was Louise's father, Louise who had been in my class since the first grade, and I wanted him to be my father. I wanted to steal him from her.

From the beginning I had gone into Louise's house like a thief. There was a huge oil painting in the front hallway with giant letters arranged on it to spell the word "LOVE." I looked at the painting and thought "yes." I remember all the details of that house, the material on the couches, the white wool rugs, the curves in walls and furniture, because I wanted it all. I remember the details of Louise's body—the first hair under her arms, the freckles on her chest when she got tan—because I wanted to inhabit that body, to be the person whose father was Mr. D.

I spent the night at Louise's house, in the trundle bed next to her. She had an asthma attack in the middle of the night. She wheezed and moaned. Her father came to take care of her. He talked to her and gave her medicine. It seemed unusual to me that her father came, not her mother (I didn't know that her mother was an alcoholic). I was annoyed that Louise had to get sick, because she was getting so much attention that I was left out. But if she were really sick, if she died, I'd get her father all to myself.

Because of my desire that everything that was Louise's be mine, everything I saw in that house was a lesson. As we grew I learned what Louise knew: I learned about the stages of Mondrian's painting, from figures to abstractions; I learned about the German expressionists and how they were different from the French impressionists. I knew how to tell the difference between a reproduction and an original. I learned about triptychs and oils and pastels and charcoal. I learned that the most beautiful art was French. Mr. D would walk us up and down the gallery that led from the main house to the new addition, telling us about each painting and each artist. In the same way he'd walk us through the woods and teach us the names of the plants. Everything he said stuck.

In the basement of the D's house, next to the wood-paneled room where Louise and I watched Bonanza on Sunday night, was a storage room whose walls were lined with shelves. The shelves were covered with boxes. There were gray boxes with the name of the D department store printed on them in red, and red boxes with the D department store name written in gray. There were boxes big enough for a toaster and small enough for a ring. No matter what size present Louise was giving, she always had the perfect box to wrap it in.

Louise was painfully shy, and I brought her out. Other kids thought she was a snob; they were afraid of her. But I would get her to talk to me. She told me all about her father, what he liked, how to please him. She let me in on her passion for art and suffering, her sense of manners and how we should behave. She wrote my mother perfect-thank you notes on Crane's stationery every time she spent the night at my house. Louise's favorite painting at the Art Institute was Rembrandt's *Lucretia*: a blood-stained woman pointing a sword at her own heart as she rang for her servant with her free hand. (Louise looked like Lucretia, with shining brown hair, translucent skin, and a fine Roman nose.) *Lucretia* became my favorite painting, too.

We spent more and more time with Louise's father. He seemed to like our company better than anybody else's. Louise wanted to share him with me, her friend who didn't have a father. Even when he wasn't with us, we would plan all day how we would tell him what we were doing. We would spend the day shopping in the D family department store: Louise would have the D's charge card, and when she showed it the sales people would be nice to her and act flustered. I would buy a lipstick or stockings to be in on it, and then the driver would take us back to her house. We'd unwrap all the packages, together, in front of Mr. D, telling him the story of each purchase. He'd always educate us, pointing out the new package design, asking us if we had spotted the undercover shoplifting detectives at the store; his favorite was a woman who dressed like a bum.

On New Year's Eve when Louise and I were twelve, Mr. D left his grownup's party in the main house. He came with a bottle of champagne into the living room of the guest wing where we were staying. It was my first taste of champagne. Mr. D told us it was important to get used to drinking. Soon we would go on dates. The boys would drink too much, and it would be our responsibility to drive them home. Louise and I drank the champagne until we were both dizzy. I woke up with a headache. At 9 A.M. on New Year's Day, I stumbled into the living room of the guest wing. I looked out the huge picture window. Mr. D was galloping on a horse on the field below. His horse took a jump over a wooden fence right below the window. I had a perfect view.

He looked sturdy. I could count on Mr. D not to die.

When I got my acceptance letter from the Collège du Léman, I called Mr. D. That same day, a bottle of perfume was delivered to my house by Mr. D's driver. Joy perfume.

I sent cards to Mr. D during the year—one from Milan, where my class went on a weekend trip. He wrote back to say that Milan had one of the most beautiful cathedrals in Europe. "I am surprised that you didn't climb up to the top and take your whole group along. You have the energy and I think you missed a good opportunity to show them what a good sightseer you are." At Christmas I wrote him and enclosed notes to him from my friends at school. "I loved your letter," he wrote back, "and I enjoyed hearing from all your friends." On Valentine's Day I got a card with a puppy dog on it, signed "anonymous" in his hand.

In March I wrote him that I would be in Paris with my mother for spring vacation. Was there any chance he would be there, too? He wrote back right away, sending me an official itinerary of his vacation with Mrs. D—two weeks in the Riviera and a week in Paris. He hoped I would get in touch if my dates overlapped with his: "I would love to see you. It would be especially nice to have you go walking around Paris with me." He added that Louise and her sister would be in Aspen for spring vacation: "I am sure she will have a good time but I know she will miss not having you there."

But I knew I wouldn't miss her. Mr. D and I were going to scale the cathedrals together!

My day with Mr. D in Paris was the best thing that happened to me when I was fifteen. I left my mother back in the Latin Quarter with the Vanderveers. I crossed to the Right Bank in a cab. The lobby of the Ritz Hotel where he stayed was drenched in a golden light. Mr. and Mrs. D greeted me in the living room of a vast suite, Mrs. D in a tapestry bergère, Mr. D on his feet, Michelin Green Guide in hand. Mr. D asked me to telephone the lobby for a phone number. The concierge on the other end of the phone dictated a long number to me, and I got the number right, realizing that the French have a different word for 70 than the Swiss. Mr. D said, "I asked you to call because your French is better than mine." I lived off that idea for a long time, the idea that my French was better than Mr. D's and that I could be useful to him because of it.

Mr. D and I said goodbye to Mrs. D for the day and walked to the nearest metro. Mr. D bought a booklet of first-class tickets. It was my first time in the metro and I hadn't known there were first- and second-class tickets. First class was empty. I was sure we were the only people in Paris who were riding first class that day.

We saw a day student from the Collège du Léman at the Tomb of the Unknown Soldier. "He's with his parents," I thought, "and I'm with Mr. D." I looked at his parents with him, I looked at Mr. D with me. There were so many tourists I couldn't see the tomb. I didn't care about the tomb. We crossed the river to the Sainte Chapelle. We stood still in its center. The stained glass windows turned the air around us a saintly blue. On the Left Bank of the river, we went to the art gallery whose phone number I had gotten for Mr. D. The owner greeted him enthusiastically in English. Mr. D informed her that he was with me, a whiz in French. She was to speak to us only in French. After we had seen the painting he was considering adding to his collection, we crossed the street to a boutique favored by Louise and Mrs. D. Mr. D said I could have whatever I wanted. I knew it was rude to want anything extravagant, so I chose a scarf. It was a *carré* (a small square), rather than a longer *foulard*, in gold and blue. We bounded toward the Jeu de Paume next, where the impressionist paintings used to be kept before they redid the Gare d'Orsay. Mr. D was an indefatigable walker; he loved to walk in the woods and he loved to walk in cities even better. I could barely keep up with him, as he would walk and point and talk, like a guide. There was nothing he liked better than to show Paris to a young person for the first time.

We stood in front of Manet's *Olympia* in the Jeu de Paume.

"Look at that painting, what do you see?"

I saw a naked woman lying on a couch with her black maid standing behind her:

"A woman, lying on her side with no clothes on and another woman in back of her, a maid, holding flowers."

"Now, look at the colors. What color is the couch?"

"White."

"Is it just one white?"

The painting had a zillion different kinds of white in it, beige gray snow ivory. As soon as I began looking for all the different whites, the painting changed utterly. The picture itself dissolved, but the paint came alive and I could see the brush strokes, see that a person had been there, working, to make the illusion.

Seeing the painting change like that before my eyes made me feel sharp-sighted; I felt I was getting to the substance of my vision, to the meaning of it. I attributed my new eyes to Mr. D and also to the city of Paris, which seemed to be organized for looking. I had never been in a place where there was so much to observe: the benches, the wrought-iron balconies, the long cars that looked like bugs, the policemen with their huge caps, the food sold outdoors, bookstalls outside along the river. Everywhere I went, there was a new tableau to take in.

Mr. D and his wife took me and my mother to dinner that night. He ordered a special soufflé for dessert that came out high in the waiter's hand; when I put my spoon in it all the whites from the Manet painting came staring up at me, and I ate the truth and light of impressionism in my soufflé.

Mr. D and his wife left for the Riviera where they were going to look at more paintings and Mrs. D would get to spend some time on the beach. I was in Paris with my mother, Mrs. Vanderveer, Priscilla, and Johnny. How can I say it was still as vivid a place, as powerful as the Paris I shared with Mr. D? I'd be lying. I've looked in my memory for the remains of the other Paris of that spring, and the first thing I found was the back of Mrs. Vanderveer's neck. She had a gray poodle hairdo cut short and lines on her neck, which she held firm and determined. She led with her neck and we, her scout troop, followed. I was used to looking at her neck because she drove Priscilla and me to school in her VW bug, Priscilla sat next to her in the front, I sat in the back seat behind her, and in France I ended up behind her again. Mrs. Vanderveer's Paris was the Paris of her own junior year abroad at Smith College—the Latin Quarter, and poetry in bookstores—but she didn't give into it, she didn't indulge in nostalgia around us. She bit her nails, which was the only sign that there was a lot on her mind, and that we weren't always easy to take around. We were on a budget; we would prowl the streets, her sure gray head in the lead, stopping in front of the restaurants, studying the plats du jour that were described on a sheet of paper posted in front. One day Priscilla and I got permission to buy our lunch at the street market on the rue de Seine and what we thought we had identified as fried chicken turned out to be eggplant: our first taste of eggplant. We wouldn't have known it was eggplant if Mrs. Vanderveer hadn't been there to explain: that's eggplant, which is "aubergine" in French and also British English.

My mother was sick with an ulcer and a spastic colon. The medicine she took made her slow and dreamy. Her eyes were unfocused. I wasn't sure she knew where she was. "Mom!" I kept turning around while walking to make sure we didn't lose her. I was afraid we might lose her. Johnny was easily distracted, too. Priscilla and I were restless. I must have spent a lot of time looking down at the street, knowing

Mrs. Vanderveer was in the lead, because along with the back of her neck I remember cobblestones—cobblestones on steep streets that wound around. From my day with Mr. D I remember sky, and clouds, and the caps on monuments.

Mrs. Vanderveer had all the train schedules mastered for our trip to the south of France. From the train window I watched the landscapes change, from the gray roofs of Paris to the blue slate roofs of the Loire and then the red roofs of the Midi. The land got craggier, hillier, like a painting by Cézanne: cubes of space overlapping.

Mrs. Vanderveer had organized a strategy for getting us and our baggage off the train within the time constraint of the three-minute stop. My mother wasn't strong enough to carry hers and we didn't have time to make two trips up and down the corridor of the train. Johnny threw all the bags out the train window; Priscilla and I were waiting to catch them from the *quai*.

We switched to a rental car. We visited Gallo-Roman ruins, including an enormous aqueduct. We drove to Avignon, where nine popes had lived in exile from Rome. We drove through the town of Grasse, dedicated to growing flowers for perfume: my Joy perfume had started in those fields. Mrs. Vanderveer read us salient facts from the Blue Guide.

"Augustus and the minister to Louis XV lived here."

"When Smollett passed this way he described it as 'very inconsiderable, and indeed in a ruinous condition,' but he was well-lodged, and 'treated with more politeness than we had met with in any other part of France.'"

"Bullet holes from World War II strafing can be observed on the northeast corner of the cathedral."

"A dam had burst here in 1959, claiming 420 victims."

There was no inch of unknown territory; even the history of visits to the town over the centuries had been recorded. You had to think about France like a cubist, in overlapping layers.

When we got to Cannes, Priscilla and I went straight to the shopping district and got identical two-piece bathing suits in an orange and pink flowered cotton. We snuck down to the water where we met two Italian boys, waiting for girls like us. The song "Hippy hippy dove vai?" was number one on Radio Monte Carlo. We lay on the rocks with the Italian boys and listened to the song. The air was warm and dry. The rocks were hot. The boys knew other boys who walked by, looked at us, murmuring phrases in Italian that made the boys laugh deep pleasurable laughs. That night, after a sensible dinner with Johnny and the mothers, we snuck out again.

"I'm gonna tell where you girls are going," Johnny threatened. We ignored him. I was wearing a sleeveless knit dress, blue and yellow stripes. It was as many inches above the knees as the Collège allowed. The Italian boy ran his hands down the sides of the dress and asked me how old I was. I told him I was fifteen and he laughed; he said he was twenty. He looked much older to me, creased, with beard stubble. He seemed reluctant to touch me after he found out I was fifteen. "I should have lied," I thought. I ran back to the hotel with Priscilla, up over the sea wall in the dark, giggling all the way because we were so late. We walked into the hotel room where our mothers had been waiting for us; my mother's voice was high and shrill and tragic and Mrs. Vanderveer's low and firm and final. Priscilla apologized. She looked sheepish and sincere. I was already calculating our next escape: I couldn't wipe the devious look off my face or apologize to my mother, whose panicked voice made me want to bolt. Priscilla and her mother always looked so normal to me; they acted the way mothers and teenage daughters were supposed to act. Was I a worse teenager than Priscilla, I wondered, or was Priscilla a better liar, feigning her daughterly affection?

A few days later, I ate a bouillabaisse with my mother, alone, after the Vanderveers had left for England: a conciliatory bouillabaisse, big clawed shellfish, spicy red out of the same pot. It was hard to get my mother to eat without thinking of her ulcer, and I was still on my breadcrust diet, but France had gotten to both of us—its pleasure principle—and our separate abnegations had broken down in sync. The bouillabaisse involved a ritual of croutons, *aioli*, special thin forks for penetrating mussels, bibs to encourage carefree manners. We went at the bouillabaisse with total determination. She forgot she was sick; I forgot I was angry. We put away the whole pot.

Coming Home

In June I took the plane home. I could feel the French sticking in my throat, the new muscles in my mouth. I had my ear open, on the plane, for the sounds of anyone speaking French because those were my sounds now. I was full of French, it was holding me up, running through me, a voice in my head, a tickle in my ear, likely to be set off at any moment. A counter language. When I got off the plane the American English sounded loud and thudding—like an insult or a lapse of faith. I would have to go hunting for French sounds, if I wanted to keep going.

It wasn't easy. People's voices sounded stretched and whiny—because of the diphthongs, I suppose. There was no control, no rhythm in the language I heard. At the airport in New York everyone was yelling and honking. The noise kept on in my head when I got home to the Midwest, where the streets were quiet. When I spoke I felt like I was outside my own body, listening to someone else, and translating. I felt small and neat and the people around me looked messy. In bed at night I felt exposed, because there was no bunk over me. No loudspeaker to wake me up. No reason to get up.

I squeezed my French toothpaste tube dry to make it last all summer. I doled out my Klorane "shampooing au henné" (for auburn highlights) in tiny portions. I lived in my tailored size 38 white cotton shirt, the kind the Lebanese girls wore. I kept my last pack of Swiss "Camel Filtres" ("un paquet de Camel Filtres, s'il vous plaît") after the last cigarette was smoked. These objects were my proof that I had lived in Europe. I had my orange and pink two-piece bathing suit from Cannes; my Bled's grammar and my Cahier de composition, filled with verb conjugations, homework assignments, and the record of my diet; on my finger I wore the Libyan gold ring that Pam gave me. M. Frichot had awarded me a copy of *Les Fleurs du mal* at the end of the term. He inscribed it "à la meilleure élève du 10ème" (to the best student in the tenth). He cut out the poems I wasn't ready for yet.

My brother was home from college. He said he didn't recognize me because I was so thin. He approved. When he saw me sulking around the house, he handed me a book about the Black Panthers: "Here. Read about struggle. Read about people with real problems." The Panthers had discovered an obscure California law that gave them the right to carry guns, thereby protecting themselves against the racist, violent police force of Oakland, California. They posed for photographs wearing guns and berets.

Mary invited me to Lake Minnetonka for a boat ride. We ran into Ted on his boat—fiberglass with a big outboard motor. He hadn't written me since confessing his love for Mary a month after I left for Switzerland. Mary had dumped him in April for David Bateman. He was dating Sue now. A hundred stories had transpired among my friends during the school year. I couldn't keep track. According to my well-rehearsed fantasy, Ted was supposed to fall in love with me again the minute he saw me, thin and exotic in my French bathing suit, exactly as we had imagined it together in the cemetery the previous summer. Instead, he looked embarrassed. I froze.

I was seized with an enormous hunger; it was summer, and I would go swimming by myself in Lake Harriet and come home and eat Wonder Bread with margarine and cinnamon sugar on top of it until I didn't feel so small and neat anymore.

At a lawn party at Mary's I discovered that my classmates had new rituals: drinking from flasks, smoking pot in the bushes, talking about rock concerts. I felt formal in my tailored white shirt. I stood watching them, twisting Pam's gold ring around my ring finger.

Steve, a serious senior, offered me a tab of synthetic mushrooms: "Don't worry, it's a mellow trip—perfect for your first time." I spent the first six hours after taking the drug in a coffee shop with Steve, rehearsing our philosophies of life while the buzz came on. I spent the rest of the night perched on my bedspread reading *Les Fleurs du mal*. Steve had said I would have visions. I didn't see much—the world was covered in a slimy green film that came from having stayed too long under the fluorescent lights in the coffee shop. But I heard noises. I heard the light bulb buzzing in my room. I heard the plaster creaking under the wallpaper. I heard every syllable of my own thoughts echoing back at me as I read Baudelaire's "Invitation au voyage": "où es-tu, où es-tu, où es-tu???" Where was I? The next day I had the sensation of having lived for a hundred years in one night. I felt thin again. Empty.

"You look so world-weary!" My mother was driving me to

a needlepoint workshop at the Edina Needlepoint Emporium, to help me stop smoking. I concentrated on filling holes with colored wool, slow and steady.

Louise was home from boarding school for the summer. I thought she would understand me. She, too, had a year behind her that no one at home could share. We sat on the floor of her room and chain-smoked until my stomach got queasy. We didn't talk about loneliness. We complained about our bodies. She told me at her school the girls took Ex-Lax if they ate too much so they wouldn't gain weight. I told her I wrote down every bite I ate, every day, in French. She told me she had a rule always to leave half the food on her plate, no matter what the portion. I told her I took the center out of the bread and only ate the crust.

Mr. D and Louise invited me to the D family cabin at Lake Azur, in the north of the state. I got to sit next to Mr. D on the private plane. He told me his latest business plan: a chain of bookstores, a new corporate logo, money from his profits for the arts. Louise and I tried to stay on our diets at Lake Azur, in spite of the cook's famous onion rings and steak. Mr. D took us water skiing, rowing, fishing, walking. He wanted us to be better friends to each other than we were. We were skimming the surface.

I returned to my school in the fall in my new role as the girl who had been away to Switzerland. At the annual French Chapel I got to read the story of the birth of Jesus in French, showing off my new accent. My teachers were impressed at my "r" and the way my intonation rose and fell. A representative had come from Vassar College to tell us that students there could design their own courses of study; one boy had lived six months in a teepee in order to understand the life of indigenous Americans. Vassar had a policy of admitting "unusual students" after the junior year. They admitted me.

I was a freshman in 1971, the height of the Vietnam War. I took courses in political science and economics, telling myself I wanted to understand what had gone wrong in the country. I tried to concentrate on the charts in Samuelson's Economics, guns on one curve and butter on another, but I couldn't. French was what I was good at. I had a stack of purple and white *Nouveaux Classiques Larousse* on the floor of my dormitory; I was in a survey course of French theater from the Middle Ages to the Theater of Cruelty. In the dorm, my friends were passing around a book of Eastern Philosophy for Westerners called *Be Here Now*. "I don't want to be here now!" I told my roommate. I hated the idea of living in the moment.

I left Vassar at the end of my freshman year to join my sister in Berkeley. I knew I was going to like it as soon as I stepped off the plane. The air was easier to breathe, cool and dry. On the way home from the airport, my sister stopped at the Black Muslim bakery to get us muffins for our breakfast. There were people in the bakery wearing fezzes, saris, earrings as long as their necks, long robes, and short leather jackets. The world was bigger here than at Vassar, filled with people who had their own ideas about how to live. You could see across the Bay Bridge to San Francisco and across the Golden Gate Bridge to Mount Tamalpais. The horizon was bigger here. My sister arranged for me to live in a grass-matted Japanese teahouse in back of the house she rented. I did political work to meet people. I worked for the April Coalition City Council campaign, the McGovern for President campaign, and for Bobby Seale, member of the Black Panther Party, when he ran for mayor of Oakland. At

Panther headquarters I met Ann Smock, who taught French literature at Berkeley. I learned from her that Jean Genet had been in New Haven to support the Panthers during their 1971 trial. Students and faculty at Yale had gone on strike in solidarity. It was a revelation to me that literature could be political—mastering the guns and butter charts might not be the only way to change the world.

I enrolled in Ann Smock's contemporary poetry course in the spring of my sophomore year. She talked about literature in a way that I recognized from my private experience of reading but had never heard articulated. She didn't worship literature as "high art" the way my high school English teachers did. She didn't drop names. She entered the poem she was teaching. She showed us around. She was baffled by literature, amused by it, suspicious of it. Literature is essential to survival and impossible to understand. Literature lies and tells the truth about lying. Writing is the opposite of making something present, I learned from her. Writing is effacement. I say: a flower! and there rises the one that is absent from all bouquets. The paraphrase is from Mallarmé's "Crise de vers" (crisis in poetry), which she taught us. There were poems in French that were nothing but love affairs with the layers of meaning of a single word over time, she told us. For a French poet the Littré dictionary was more essential than having a soul: the dictionary was the soul of poetry.

I got so wrapped up in a point she was making about the Littré that I lit the filter end of my cigarette. Everyone in the class laughed when they noticed. I took the cigarette out of my mouth so I could laugh with them. I had been so intent on the idea of the dictionary that for a moment I had forgotten myself. I had unlearned my most automatic habit in my relationship to the object world; it was exhilarating to be distracted by ideas.

In Francis Ponge's *Le Parti pris des choses*, I found an expression of the overlapping spheres of words and things. Ponge chose the most ordinary objects as the subjects of his poems—the oyster, the orange, and the cigarette. Each of his objects is a worker, sweating and straining to make its place in the world. Language speaks about itself through them. The oyster, in French—*l'huître*—is spelled with a circumflex accent marking the place where, as recently as the Renaissance, there used to be an "s"—*uistre*. *Huître*, the word, hides an "s"; *huître*, the object, hides a pearl. Ponge's oyster poem was peppered with words containing circumflexes, all of them necessary to describe the object: "blanchâtre" (the whitish oyster shell); "opiniâtrement" (the stubbornly closed oyster), "verdâtre" (the slimy greenish sack inside), "noirâtre" (the black lacy fringe edging the oyster meat). I understood from Ponge why I could lose myself in language. Why I could read the same sentences over and over, different meanings or possibilities coming to the surface each time:

> *Parfois très rare une formule perle à leur gosier de nacre, d'où l'on trouve aussitôt à s'orner.*

Sometimes, very rarely, a saying pearls forth from their nacreous throats; we get to decorate ourselves.

I am walking down a road in Versoix. I know I'm in Switzerland because the road is antiseptically clean. I could eat on this street. I've bought a piece of Malabar brand bubble gum from the tabac. I am proud of my conversation with the storekeeper. She is ruddy and round.

Each of her transactions is utterly formulaic. I've said the right words, as though buying a piece of gum in French were totally normal. I've said "Je vous remercie, Madame" (I know the verb "remercier," meaning "to thank"; I know how to conjugate my thank-you's now, instead of saying a simple "merci"). I open the Malabar wrapper, revealing a cartoon tattoo on the inside. Directions say it can be transferred to any surface using water. I spit on the cartoon as I walk. I roll up my sleeve. I slap the cartoon onto my arm in the spot where I get vaccinations. The tattoo takes. I'm marked. I use so much spit that the outline of the tattoo streaks. I stop to examine my upper arm. It's a mush of red and blue and yellow. I can't read it.

I stayed up all night working on my final project for Ann Smock's poetry class: a book of prose poems, including language dreams, etymologies, collages of advertisement snippets, and bilingual puns. I turned in the poems as my final paper. I was buzzing with energy and creative satisfaction.

A phone call from Louise took me by surprise. She was celebrating the end of her first year at Vassar. There was tension in our conversation from the beginning:

"Who are you hanging out with?"
"Trip Murphy."
"Oh yeah, I knew that guy. Sort of a snob."
"Maybe to you."
[silence]
"What's California like?"
"It's great, I'm in this poetry class and I'm in the movement here. You know, fighting capitalist pigs."

The phrase slid out before I realized what I had said.

"How dare you! How dare you talk about capitalist pigs after all my father has done for you!"

Louise was usually so reserved. I had never heard her raise her voice to anyone.

"Louise! I wasn't talking about your father."
"Well, who were you talking about then? He IS a capitalist. And you're saying that capitalists are pigs."
"Louise!"

It was one of those conversations that should have had subtitles, making clear what we were really arguing about. For example:

"I shared him with you!"
"You'd never tell him anything. All he wanted was to talk with someone who would really talk to him. No wonder he liked me better."
"He's my father, not yours. Don't you ever forget it."
"You don't even appreciate him. If I had a father like him . . ."
"How much do you appreciate him? You acted like he was your father. He took you to Aspen, he showed you Paris. And now, suddenly he's a 'capitalist pig.' How dare you!"

She was right—I hadn't written to Mr. D for two years, I hadn't thanked him. He had taught me to be active, not just brood about life, and I was being active in Berkeley. It would have been hard to explain to him exactly what I was doing, but I should have tried. I could have risked it.

Whenever I thought about the Ds in the years that passed before I finally wrote to Mr. D, a single painting would flash into my head in its exact details *in situ*: the red, yellow, and blue Mondrian, hanging over a white love seat in the D living room. A needlepoint pillow stitched to match the design of the painting was propped on the left cushion of the love seat.

On a summer night when Louise and I were sixteen, Louise, her brothers and sister, Mr. and Mrs. D, and I played a game called "trust," with the Mondrian—its rigorous straight lines and demand for balance and harmony— staring us in the face. Six of us interlocked our hands in a net. The seventh player let herself fall onto us, taking the risk, feeling the support. We formed another net, and another, until each of us had had the sensation, both of supporting a falling player and of being the one who falls.

Three years later I walked into the waiting room at the San Francisco airport, a newly declared "French major." Ann Smock was sending me off on my junior year abroad with a present—Raymond Queneau's *Le Journal de Sally Mara*, the intimate diary of an Irish schoolgirl, written in fractured French (Queneau, a wicked parodist, had perfected the way French might be butchered by an anglophone adolescent). I was part Queneau, part Sally Mara; part precocious student spoofing my own lessons, part enthused adolescent wanting to please her teacher. Ann acknowledged both sides: "Here," she had said when she handed me the book, "you'll like these language games."

I sat in the airport lounge, examining my fellow students over the top of the beige Gallimard/nrf book jacket that I held in front of my face like a flag. I wanted the other students on the program to see that I was no tourist. I was going to live in France.

Part Three: *Getting It Right*

André

I met André at the first party of the year in Pau, where our junior-year-abroad group had a six-week orientation before settling down in Bordeaux. He came bounding into the room at me. He was long and wiry with shiny black hair and a devil smile on his face. He sat me down on the couch, put one hand on each of my shoulders: "Alors, ma petite américaine, tu t'appelles comment?" The room was packed with noisy foreign students. André's voice drowned them out completely. "Serre-moi," he said, taking his arms off my shoulders and holding them out toward me. I didn't know those words in French but I figured out exactly what they meant from André's body: "Serre-moi" meant "hold me." Ten minutes later I went with him into the nearest bedroom—I was in love with my own recklessness—and he put his shirt on a lamp for just the right amount of light. We got into bed and his shirt caught on fire. It was like that with him, sudden blazes; he was always jumping up to put out some fire or other, leaping and howling at his own antics. His main activities were mountain climbing (the Pyrenees), painting, and chasing women. He was twenty-seven and he worked for a graphic arts firm, but it was impossible to think of him as an office worker.

I used to wait for him to come into the café around seven. He entered the room like a mannequin, one shoulder slightly behind the other and his legs in front of him. His smile was subtle and controlled; no teeth showed. He had a way of stopping to survey the room before coming over to my table that made me hold my breath for fear he wouldn't come. He looked down his greyhound nose at each of my girlfriends, bent his long frame forward to give the ceremonial kiss on each cheek, all around the table. I was last. I got four kisses, two on each cheek, with the same geometric precision.

I liked to watch André sitting across from me at the café, smoking his cigarette with his head tilted to one side to show off his cheek bones. He exuded an Egyptian beauty, his jet black hair bouncing off his shoulders, his long muscles showing through his skin. There was so much energy in that body, it seemed to be in motion even when he was sitting.

He was a moralist and he had theories. He talked about his "aesthetic folly"—his drunken outings—and about "the bourgeois complacency" of most women (their desire for commitment and stability; his love of freedom). He thought American women talked too much, but he liked me because I was natural. Although I shouldn't wear so much black.

I kept a diary and I started taking notes on André: "André ate a dead bee he found on the steps of a church."

I liked to watch him. I studied André showering. He scrubbed every inch of himself with a soapy washcloth that he wrapped around his hand like an envelope. I watched him washing, I watched all his muscles under the soap, especially the ones around his chest he'd got from climbing mountains. I thought to myself, this is the way a man showers when he only gets a shower once a week. I thought of all the men I knew who showered every day, sloppily, and who had nothing to wash off.

I went to classes, part of our six-week orientation to French culture. In class I spent a lot of time with my head on the desk, nothing but André in it. I went to the language lab for phonetic testing and they said I was starting to get the regional Gascon accent in my "r"s, I should watch out. I had been studying André too hard.

We read André Bazin and learned the difference between Hollywood film and the French *cinéma d'auteur*, film so marked by the style of its director you can say it has an author, like a book. One day we were all bused to the Casino in Pau, to watch Alain Resnais and Marguerite Duras's *Hiroshima mon amour* on a big screen. The movie begins with lovers, a French actress and a Japanese architect. In the first frames, you see their bodies close up, their sweat mixed with shiny sprinkles that look like ash—the ash of the atomic bomb in Hiroshima. I watched their bodies and I heard their voices. The dialogue is sparse in this movie, the sentences are as simple as sentences in a first-year language text, except that they are erotic. One staccato statement after another, the pronoun "tu"—the familiar "you"—in every sentence. The movie taught me what "tu" means, how intimate, how precious—"You are like a thousand women together," he says, and she: "That is because you don't know me." The sentences are so bare that they seem to mean everything—a thousand sentences packed together in a few words, every sentence an unexploded bomb. She: "You speak French well." He: "Don't I. I'm happy you've finally noticed" (laughter). After it was over, I still felt inside the bare secret world of the movie and went to sit in a park, where I wrote to André in an erotic trance. "When I lose my words in French," I wrote, "a radical transformation occurs. My thoughts are no longer thoughts, they are images, visions. More important—the feeling of power in not being able to communicate, the feeling of being stripped down to the most fundamental communication. I am with you, I see black and then flashes: a leg, a sex, a nose. Seen, felt, tasted. The taste of your body pursues me," I wrote. "Like an essence."

But André wasn't buying it. I still have the letter, stuck between the pages of my diary from that year; it has his corrections all over it. Where I wrote "la joie de la reverse," which is made-up French for "the joy of reversal," he crossed it out and wrote "the joy of anti-conformism." (One of his slogans about himself was that he was an anti-conformist.)

This should have been my first clue that what I really wanted from André was language, but in the short run all it did was make me feel more attached to him, without knowing why I was attached. I can still hear the sound he made when he read my love letter: "T,t,t," with that little ticking sound French people make by putting the tips of their tongues on the roof of their mouths—a fussy, condescending sound, by way of saying, "that's not how one says it." What I wanted more than anything, more than André even, was to make those sounds, which were the true sounds of being French, and so even as he was insulting me and discounting my passion with a vocabulary lesson, I was listening and studying and recording his response.

He decided to take me out for a ninety-six-franc meal, for my education. *Tripes à la mode de Caen*—the stomach of some animal, and the *spécialité de la maison.* I ate it in huge bites, to show him I wasn't squeamish. Before he had too much to drink he made a speech at me, in his high moral style: "You represent the woman I would like to love if I were older and if I dominated myself. I am very happy to have known you. But I want a woman I can express myself with. You understand my words but not my language—you don't even realize how great a problem it is between us." (I wrote the whole speech down in my diary afterwards, word for word.) He tried to pronounce the difference between "word" and "world" in English—he thought it was funny they were so alike, and that their similarity had to do with us, with our problem. He couldn't make the "l" sound in "world." He ordered schnapps for two plus a cognac, then another. He drank them all. We raced off to a disco in his Deux Chevaux. He leaped out under the strobe lights, out of my sight. I stood outside the dancing *piste* and watched him sidle up to four different women, one after another, twirling each of them around him in his own athletic interpretation of "le rock." His sister was at the discothèque. She advised me to grab him and start making out with him if I wanted to get home. Twice on the way home he stopped the car to weep in my lap, sobbing giant tears.

The next day I got a note that said: "I'm sorry Alice. Hier soir j'avais trop bu. J'espère que tu ne m'en tiendras pas rigueur. Tendresse. André." Which means: "I drank too much last night. Don't be too hard on me." I received this note like a haiku and pasted it in my diary.

That week I kept running over his speech in my mind. What was the difference between his words and my words, his world and my world? When I said a French word, why wasn't it the same as when he said one? What could I do to make it be the same? I had to stick it out with him, he was transmitting new words to me every day and I needed more. In fact, while Barbara and Buffy and Kacy (André dubbed us "l'équipe"—the team) rolled their eyes about what a raw deal I was getting from this creep, I was all the more determined to be with him. He was in all my daydreams now. I wanted to crawl into his skin, live in his body, be him. The words he used to talk to me, I wanted to use back. I wanted them to be my words.

The last weekend I spent with André, we went to a sleazy hotel in Toulouse. He was on another drinking binge and we both got bitten up by bedbugs—or so I thought at the time. When I got back to the dorm my neck was swollen and my ear was all red. I was hot, and I went into a long sleep that I thought was due to exhaustion from being with André. Within forty-eight hours the swelling on my neck felt like a tumor and the whole side of my face was swollen. My right eye was shut. I hid in my dorm room. When I had to go for a meal I wrapped my neck in a scarf and put a hat down over my right eye. I was almost too sick to care that André was spending the night down the hall from me with Maïté, a French woman who was one of the assistants in charge of orienting us. She was part Basque, like him, and lanky like him, only softer; she dressed in Indian prints and sheepskin vests.

The doctors didn't really know what was wrong with me, so they did tests. They tried one medicine, then another. Finally they sent me to a convent, where I got free antibiotic shots in my behind daily. I went there every day for seven days to get rid of the infection. The stark white cot where I submitted to the treatment, the nuns' quiet efficiency, had a soothing effect on me. I was cleansed by charity.

When I came out of the worst of my sickness I thought about it like this: it was the two of them against me. Two people who had the words and shared the world and were busy communicating in their authentic language, and me, all alone in my room. Maïté had something I couldn't have, her blood and her tongue and a name with accents in it. I was burning with race envy.

I spent a lot of time reading, and sitting in cafés with "l'équipe," my team of girlfriends, and writing in my diary about André and what he meant. He wanted me to be natural, and I wanted him to make me French. When I thought back on the way the right side of me had swelled up, my neck and my ear and my eye, it was as if half of my face had been at war with that project. Half of me, at least, was allergic to André.

The day our group left for Bordeaux, André and Maïté were standing together at the bus stop and André gave me the ceremonial cheek kiss right in front of her, and whispered the possibility of a visit in my tender but healed ear. I could count on his infidelity working both ways.

In Bordeaux we signed up for housing with Monsieur Garcia, the administrative assistant of the University of California program. "You can live with a family or you can have liberty," Garcia said. A family meant nice quarters and no visitors; liberty meant scruffier quarters. Everyone knew that liberty really meant liberty to have sex, and life in France without sex was inconceivable to me.

André showed up in Bordeaux two or three times that year, strictly on the run. Once he claimed he was in town doing a two-week *stage* (the French term for a mini-apprenticeship) on bug extermination with his friend Serge.

He rang the doorbell in the middle of the night and leapt into my bed. His breath smelled like rotten fruit and he had one of those stubborn erections that doesn't even respond to sex. Finally he rolled away from me, muttering what I thought was "Je suis costaud" (I'm strong), falling into a dead sleep. After a few days of thinking about the phonetic possibilities ("choo-ee co stow" or "choo-ee co stew"?), and looking through dictionaries, I decided he had actually been saying, "je suis encore saoul" (I'm still drunk), only drunkenly: "j'suis 'co soo," as a way of explaining why he hadn't been able to come. I was still putting up with André, for his beauty and for his words.

Each room in my boardinghouse had a sink and bidet. Outside was the outhouse, with maggots. The other boarders were immigrant workers. Across the hall was Caméra, from the République of Guinée, who had a job in construction and was trying to study math on the side with do-it-yourself tapes. He helped me set up a *camping gaz* so I could make omelettes. He took me to the African Student Association dance where I started dancing with the biggest creep there. "Il ne vaut rien, " Caméra warned me, "he's worth nothing; a first-rate hustler." The hustler danced like a wild marionette and told me what he liked: "fun, acid, women, music." I made a rendezvous with him, which I didn't keep. Caméra was angry with me, and we stopped speaking.

For weeks I didn't want to open the door of my room, for fear of seeing Caméra, his disapproving glance. I kept the door to my room closed, as though some father had grounded me. When I was out I had the energy of an escaped convict; when I was home the righteousness of a cloistered nun. It felt familiar.

I had to go to the bathroom all the time. The more I

dreaded the outhouse, the more I had to go. I planned outings to cafés, to use the bathrooms there. I knew which cafés
in my part of town had clean bathrooms, with seats, and
which ones had stand-up Turkish toilets. If I timed it right I
could go to the best café in town, the Régent, anesthetize
myself with steamed milk, go to the bathroom, and make it
home for a night of dreams. When I walked home from the
café it was pitch black and sometimes a *clochard*, a bum,
yelled obscenities at me. I was too lost in my thoughts to be
scared.

The room became my world. Clean sheets once a week. I
began to recognize the people on my street: the man with
no arms, the *tabac* lady with the patchwork shawl, the old
concierge and his creaking keys, and Papillon, the pharmacist around the corner. My room and I were together now;
night and morning rituals established themselves with
pleasantly passing weeks. The bidet was no longer exotic; I
soaked my tired feet in it. I had a wool shawl that I wrapped
around my nightgowned shoulders and that transported
me into timelessness. I put the shawl on to read: *Le Père
Goriot*, about a nineteenth-century boardinghouse, and *Les
Liaisons dangereuses*, about a woman who controls her world
through letters but is destroyed in the end. My room could
exist in any century, in any French city.

The administration of the California program arranged all
kinds of outings and connections for us students. I babysat
for a rich family who lived in a modern house. Their floor
was made of polished stones. I was invited to a chateau and I
wore my best dress, ready to discuss literature. I got there
and my French hosts greeted me in sneakers. They were
growing Silver Queen corn in their backyard, and they
wanted a fourth for tennis. Of all the Americans in my group

the one they liked best was the freckled jock who could hardly speak French and went everywhere on his ten-speed bike. I was waiting to be rewarded for my good French, but he got all the attention. He was having fun playing the American mascot, while I was doing all the hard work of learning their language and what I thought were their social customs. I would have been ready to pose as the Marlboro Man to get the kind of attention he got from the French. But I had veered off in the other direction; I was trying to be French. Besides, I knew his ploy wouldn't work for me: a girl can't be a Marlboro Man.

I was always watching and pretending, pretending and watching. I met a guy from Colorado. We were sitting at the French student restaurant together and I was peeling my pear so carefully, he said, he didn't know I was American. We went to the French student restaurant to meet people but no one spoke at the table, just peeled their fruit and left. This guy (his name is gone) and I made up stories instead of going to bed together (we weren't supposed to go to bed with each other: we were on our junior year abroad). In one, I would be a prostitute who specialized in American men wanting to meet French girls. The joke would be that I wouldn't be French at all. We figured out where I would have to go and what I would wear and say, and what they would say. He would be my *proxénète*, the entrepreneur, and we would make tons of money and live well.

He went off and found a French girlfriend, a real one, and the next time I saw him they were on his moped, her arms around his waist, her hair in one of those high French pony tails waving in the breeze. When he saw me he waved proudly, a little sheepish to have me see him like that in the middle of his fantasy. I waved back and laughed.

I wanted to travel on my own, be brave, but I wasn't. I was always afraid of making a *faux pas*. I took a taxi to the train station to catch a train and I opened the taxi door just as a car was racing down the street. The car smashed into the taxi door, crumpling it. It was a fancy taxi, a top-of-the-line Renault, and the driver was screaming at me about his insurance and how much my foreigner stupidity was going to cost him. He was so disgusted he wouldn't let me pay the fare. I skulked into the station, my head hung low: this was my great adventure.

In the seventeen years since I met André, my ear has swelled up on me from time to time, although never as dramatically as that September in Pau. When I was writing this book, it happened again. The swelling came on so quickly that I went right to the doctor, who took one look at me and said, "You have herpes simplex on your ear." He'd only seen one case of herpes on the ear in all his years of medical practice: a man who had the cold sore on his mouth kissed his wife on the ear, and she got the virus.

As I searched back in my mind, I could see the tiny little blister on André's upper lip, a neat imperfection I was determined to ignore but that turned into his legacy. My precious ear, my radar, my antenna: the locus of my whole attraction to French, and André went right for it! Maybe he bit me there, maybe he kissed me, or maybe he just whispered some of his words with his lip up against my earlobe, and the virus took.

At the time, when I thought about him and Maïté, I thought, "It's because my French isn't good enough" and "It's because she's French." When he told me I couldn't understand his language, André had picked the accusation I was most vulnerable to. Afterwards I thought, "I'll show him. I'll know all there is to know about his language. I'll know his language better than he does, someday."

After I had become a French professor, I wrote André, and he wrote back. The nonconformist was still living at the same address, and I had moved ten times. I felt glad about that. There were a few spelling mistakes in his letter to me, the kind I'm hired to correct. But I didn't feel gleeful about his spelling, because it hadn't been spelling that I wanted from him. I wanted to breathe in French with André, I wanted to sweat French sweat. It was the rhythm and pulse of his French I wanted, the body of it, and he refused me, he told me I could never get that. I had to get it another way.

Micheline

I went into the pharmacy near my apartment to ask for medicine for mosquito bites in my best French: "quelque chose contre les piques de moustiques" (something against . . .). But since "pique" means "spade," not "bite" ("bite" is "piqûre"), the pharmacist and I were off and running, his hilarity, my blushes, his old man Legion of Honor gallantry, and all the rest. "Please call me Papillon," he said, and he invited me to his family lunch that Saturday. I like to tell the story to students because it is about a French mistake leading to something good.

It was one of those endless meals you read about in language classes—a first course of foie gras and a second course of rabbit and french fries and a salad and a cheese course and a fancy store-bought dessert. Bottles of wine with dust still on them from the cave tucked under the pharmacy, the kind with sediment in the bottom and a ten-layered taste you can study. I was seated up at the head of the table, in close range of Papillon who teased me and told stories about his adventures in Chicago, in the twenties. "I am Veaux—veal—you understand?" he kept saying in a Maurice-Chevalier-only-more-so fractured English. He told me what it was like to sit on a park bench in Chicago and watch the girls; he raved about the American girls and how tough they were, like soldiers, with legs like bayonets. His daughter Micheline was there, across the table from me, a cautious smile set on her face. She interrupted Papillon's flights of fancy to question me in a calm pedagogical voice, every word with its beat. Her children were at the table too: Florence was deeply shy; Sylvie and François were kids, François barely out of shorts. The meal was served by a Spanish woman named Carmen, with one eye that twitched and looked askance. The apartment was filled with extravagant Lalique vases of all sizes and deco furniture, big red club chairs with arms wide enough to hold two tea cups. I walked out of there dazed, onto the street where the sun was setting over Eleanor of Aquitaine's tower, across the street. Five hours had passed.

I went back year after year to see this family from my junior year abroad in 1973–74. I went to Papillon's apartment above the pharmacy, then to Micheline's house, rue de Patay, then back to Papillon's retirement house in Pessac, for the traditional Saturday lunch. I heard many more Papillon stories: how he went to Spain with his medicines, to help the Republicans, and came back disgusted by their violence. I heard about his medals, his stamp collection, his pharmaceutical vases. I heard how he controlled pharmaceutical supplies during the Occupation. I heard about his love for the Maréchal Pétain, "who was betrayed by France." He had a scarf printed with a drawing of the island where Pétain was exiled, and a motto about France's shame. He tried to lend it to me to wear on a train trip, he thought I would get cold, but Micheline intervened, gently: "You're not going to send this poor young American girl off to Corsica with a Philippe

Pétain label around her neck." The children rolled their eyes and explained later what American children are rarely called upon to explain: the connection between family history, family prejudices, and big history, with a capital H. It would take me ten more years to figure out that if you had been a World War I veteran and not a Jew, Pétain could have been your hero in 1940. No matter how much wrong he did later, the memory of Verdun might have blinded you to it.

I think a lot about that Pétain scarf and the way Papillon wanted me to wrap up in it. I always go back to him for understanding France: the Third Republic, Gaullism, the Spanish Loyalists, French myths about the U.S. For each mystery about France I can think back to Papillon barking out some absurd slogan that would turn out to be soaked in politics, and I remember his bottles and his jars and vases like a stage set.

He was always taking things down off his shelves, as an offering: a stamp, a handkerchief, a pharmaceutical vase. Things, but always things with history. He had enough things, it seemed, to give to all Bordeaux and still there would be more.

Each of the children followed in the family's medical tradition: François became a pharmacist, Sylvie a dentist, Florence a pathologist. Papillon died in 1987; the next year François bought a pharmacy, and Sylvie married Richard. The family dog, Virginie, a puppy when I was nineteen, was blind and emaciated like a skeleton when I was thirty-four. No one could bear to put her to sleep.

I measured the passing of time by that house, that dog, as our lives mingled and meshed. They became my French family and I their American friend.

*   *   *

From the beginning I loved the fact that Micheline healed people with language troubles. "Dr. Micheline Veaux: Maladies du langage" (illnesses of language) was inscribed on a bronze plaque over her doorbell. Micheline Veaux is a *phoniatre*, a physician who specializes in problems, physical and mental, that show themselves in speech. People recovering from throat operations, stutterers, aphasiacs, immigrants with psychological traumas in their newly acquired tongue. People who, for one reason or another, speak in the wrong pitch—too high or too low—and hurt their voices. She works with them on a keyboard, and helps them find their register. Her perspective is psychoanalytic; she believes, for example, that it is dangerous to treat a symptom without treating the cause. It is dangerous to cure someone of stuttering if the stuttering fulfills a psychic need that the person hasn't understood. Language is not a machine you can break and fix with the right technique, it is a function of the whole person, an expression of culture, desire, need. Her respect for everything that is alive in speech was profoundly new to me, and it corresponded to my need to wonder about language. Inside our language is our history, personal and political. This is what Micheline showed me.

When you ring the doorbell at Micheline's house, the first sound you hear is Virginie, the dachshund, whining and scraping her nails over the tile floor in the hallway. Micheline's office is to the left of the hallway, and it is decorated in the style favored by French doctors: Empire. The furniture is straight-edged and commanding. A desk, glass-cased *étagères* full of books and toys. An analyst's couch. She is the *chef*, the boss. But not in the style of Napoleon: physically she is big, sitting behind her Empire desk, with her warrior's beaked nose, her olive skin and frosted hair. She is from the Auvergne, the Massif Central where her Protestant ancestors are buried—there is a trace in her looks of Vercingetorix, the warrior of Ancient Gaul who held off Caesar in that very region. She wears big swathes of expensive fabric, but she can't be bothered with shoes—hers look squashed. There are tape recorders around, and records, along with the children's toys, and on the wall is a model of a throat and mouth with tongue, tonsils, and teeth.

Micheline gave me one of the psychological tests she gives her patients:

"My father is a tailor," I was supposed to write. "Mon père est tailleur." But many of her patients write instead, "Mon père est ailleurs" ("My father is somewhere else.") French lets you make dramatic puns this way, because of "liaison": a fact of French pronunciation which means that a consonant at the end of one word (the "t" in "est") can hook up with the subsequent word beginning with a vowel ("ailleurs"), creating an ambiguity as to whether the word you are hearing is "ailleurs" or "tailleur." The French psychoanalyst Jacques Lacan would have appreciated Micheline's test sentence. He believed that the child gains access to language only when it perceives the existence of the father, which allows it to break out of infantile dualisms—self and mother, inside and outside. "Somewhere out there, somewhere else, is my father": this, says Lacan, is the child's inauguration into language, the symbolic order, and the law. But it is mothers, traditionally, who teach language, who listen and correct, it is mothers who are the first to hear new words. It is mothers who break or heal a child's tongue.

In spite of her testing, Micheline is not a Lacanian. "Dictation is a police state," she told me, "with grammar as the law. Dictation can ruin a child's relationship to language."

Dictation is one of the permanent rites of French education. You listen to the teacher's voice and you write down every word. For every wrong accent, every wrong verb ending, you lose points; your listening and your knowledge of the transition from voice to writing must be exquisite. Around the time that Micheline was analyzing its dangers, I was learning to give dictation in the French classes I taught. How I must love the law, I thought; how I love getting every word perfect, and now giving them and getting them back. Micheline's resistance to dictation, the deep seriousness of her critique, made the dull pedagogical exercise seem like a rebellion. She wanted me to relax with my French, to live with it. I wanted to control every word.

I went in to her office wanting to work on my French, and she recorded my voice on her tape recorder. I heard my foreign intonation, which she called my "song." "You'll never get rid of that song, " she said, "but what does it matter?" I wanted to hire her, pay her thousands of dollars, to rid me of it.

"Speech," Micheline told me, "is the highest and lowest human function, the *endroit charnière* [the hitch] between the mechanical grunt of the vocal chords and the poetry of cognition."

I met her most successful former patient, a Vietnamese boat person named, like the past participle, Vu. He no longer stuttered. One spring he came to New York and looked me up, and we walked down Riverside Drive together to Grant's Tomb. It happened to be the tenth anniversary of the fall of Saigon, April 30, 1985, and this made me feel that we ought to be together, on that day. I took him to dinner, Texas barbecue. When I was in Paris he called me. We started to compete. We got annoyed at one another. He wanted to be my French teacher. I wanted my French to be better than his. He worked for the bureau of standardization and wanted to write novels. We picked at one another—he found every wrong word I uttered—in fact we argued about the meanings of words and their usage. "His usage is standard," I thought, "merely standard." Micheline was disgusted by my lack of generosity where Vu was concerned. "Perhaps he doesn't have every quality," she told me "but you have no idea what he has been through, how he has rebuilt his life from nothing. Losing his mother and sister in a boat—we haven't a clue what that was like." I was jealous of his success, his transcendence of the worst odds, his pain conquered. It was a measly feeling.

Every time I went back to Bordeaux they told me whether or not I'd lost my French. "You've still got it." Or, "You're starting to lose it but you'll get it back." "It" seemed to depend on nothing—not whether I'd been teaching, not whether I'd been spending time with French people. Some fluke of memory and forgetting was involved. Sometimes I would call them from the States, after months of silence, and my simplest comments were unfathomable to them.

Micheline helped me study for the GRE's in French from a practice book: "Is France sometimes referred to as a pentagon, an octagon, or a hexagon?" This made us laugh, because we had traveled through the entire hexagon, Micheline and the kids and me, and in the car they had instructed me about the shape of France. Micheline's children knew the green Michelin guidebooks so well that they could imitate them effortlessly, and as we drove into the next one-horse town, François would elaborate a parody: "Autin-sur-mer, pearl of the Atlantic . . ." I learned to swear in traffic jams, listening to Micheline in the driver's seat. My family snapshots from those trips show the Châteaux of the

Loire; force-fed geese of the Dordogne; Sylvie, Micheline, and me on a bench, looking exactly alike in our posture and pose. Sometimes an American would walk into the restaurant, the hotel, the church where we were, and I felt safe and warm with my French family, protected from myself. I heard the American voices and they were foreign to me.

Not that France didn't change. France became more American every year, even as Americans longed more and more for the traditions they had lost that France still had. That was part of what we wanted in each other, in the beginning: me the ritual of France, Micheline the ease of America.

In the seventies, as the American middle class abandoned their soup cans and frozen food for lengthy recipes à la Julia Child, Micheline was moving in the opposite direction. Around the time that wine became weekly, if not daily, in American middle-class families, it disappeared from Micheline's lunch table altogether. In fact I first learned the word for "daily"— *quotidien*—at lunch when Micheline described a magazine article about "daily alcoholism" in France, the thousands of French people who were alcoholics without really knowing it, merely because of the amount of wine they drank with every meal. Around the time that instant mashed potato flakes and TV dinners became an embarrassment in bourgeois Minneapolis, they appeared in bourgeois Bordeaux. The first action she took the day after her divorce, Micheline told me, was to buy a freezer. This was her freedom.

She took me to the cafeteria at the *hypermarché*, so big it's not a super- but a hypermarket, on the outskirts of Bordeaux. The food was Woolworth's only worse, frozen veal covered in Cheese Whiz and pizza sauce. I ate with relish, this dish I would have rejected at home but which in France was exotic. The place was decorated American Western style, big painted cowboys with neon lassos. I marveled at the novel décor with my French family.

Usually we didn't go out. There was no hanging around in cafés. And then, when Papillon got too old, even the obligatory Saturday lunch at his house ended. Meals shrank. Sometimes dinner was salmon spread on packaged toast, or a piece of cheese from the glass cheese cage. Often it was only out of respect for the visiting francophiles that tradition was trotted out. Florence made a crusted fish or her endive in béchamel and a tart; François, with his pharmacist's nose, brought just the right wine from the inexhaustible cellar.

I went back there every summer, every trip, for no reason, as though it were my family. Each time, I felt the same mixture of anticipation and annoyance, as though it were my family so I had to go. I expected to be bored there, quiet. I went just to go to the same places: the bus stop at the Barrière de Pessac, the big bookstore, the street where I shopped for clothes when I was a student. I went because I needed to make sure the places were still there, to make sure I really once lived there and I was really attached to this foreign place.

There in Bordeaux is where my mouth and my eyes and my ears for France started to work. When I was fifteen and had my first conversation all in French, in Switzerland, it was a religious awakening. In Bordeaux it became regular, boring, real. *Quotidien.*

Céline

I

There was a dead rat the size of a German Shepherd puppy in the gutter in front of my boardinghouse the morning I began to read Céline's *Journey to the End of the Night*. It was pitiful, with wet slick gray-brown fur that stuck together in clumps. Since I'd never seen a rat before, this one looked sweeter and more vulnerable than I had imagined a rat to be. No teeth were showing.

Winter solstice held sway; it was still dark in the mornings when I left to take the bus from the Cathédrale St. André to the suburban University of Bordeaux campus at Talence, where "Twentieth-Century French Literature for Foreigners" met. Barbara, of "l'équipe," had given our literature professor the nickname "the Drycleaner" because of his tailored, spotless appearance, incongruous in the academic barracks at Talence: going to the bathroom was a struggle not to gag because of the violent graffiti and the shit smeared on the walls.

The Drycleaner dared us to understand Céline, whose French, he promised, offered the most idiomatic, difficult, and lively sense of the language we would get in the course of the semester, perhaps in our lives. Scenes of New York and Detroit in *Journey* might help the Americans—the majority foreign population represented in our class—through one section of the book.

What drew me first to Céline's language were wandering rhythmic phrases, like this one:

Comme si j'avais su où j'allais, j'ai eu l'air de choisir encore et j'ai changé de route, j'ai pris sur ma droite une autre rue, mieux éclairée, "Broadway" qu'elle s'appelait.

As if I knew where I was going, I put on an air of choosing and changed my direction, taking a different street on my right, one that was better lit. "Broadway" it was called.

Sundays in Bordeaux I walked alone down the Cours de l'Intendance, the Cours Victor Hugo and the Quai des Chartrons. The shops were closed, the bourgeois families locked away in their houses; the only people on the streets were foreigners—students and workers, mostly North Africans:

C'était comme une plaie triste la rue qui n'en finissait plus, avec nous au fond, nous autres, d'un bord à l'autre, d'une peine à l'autre, vers le bout qu'on ne voit jamais, le bout de toutes les rues du monde.

That street was like a dismal gash, endless, with us at the bottom of it, filling it from side to side, advancing from sorrow to sorrow, toward an end that is never in sight, the end of all the streets in the world.

What exquisite misery I felt! Disconnected, not belonging, desiring every house, imagining every happy scene behind every stone wall, taking in the lewd empty glances, given and received. Céline could express it all in a sentence through the sound of his words as much as their meaning.

When I read him I luxuriated in despair, dark thoughts, and a commitment to eternal exile.

II

The same writer who, in *Journey to the End of the Night*, wrote elegies to society's marginal characters, to foreignness and the common path towards death, came under the grip of a mad anti-Semitism in the 1930s, claiming his writing style was the expression of his pure French blood, his "native rhythm." His music was in his genes, he said; no foreigners were capable of genius. Fellow writers were nothing but Jews and robots, standardizing the language, destroying French literature.

Céline may have liberated the French language, but not himself. His most excited, violent, rhythmic, effective writing was sparked by everyday anger and resentment. His well-honed technique—developed directly from the hundreds of pages of racist diatribe he spewed out in 1937 and 1938—was to brood on a newspaper article or an attack on him until he got really steamed, picked up his pen, and let fly.

When he was most reviled in France, at the end of the German occupation, Céline's hate language was linked in the public mind to everything that had happened since France fell to the Nazis in 1940. French Jews had been stripped by the Vichy government of their professions and businesses and rights, forced to wear yellow stars on their coats, deported to Drancy and beyond, to die in German and Polish camps. French officials first deported foreign Jews, then French nationals. Seventy-six thousand Jews went to camps from France; 3 percent returned. Céline fled

Paris at the Liberation, crossed through Germany, and spent the years 1945–50 in exile in Denmark. He was tried in absentia by the French in 1950 and given amnesty in 1951 under a clause pardoning World War I veterans. The judge didn't know that the Dr. Destouches mentioned in the amnesty was the same man as the writer "Céline."

In 1974, my junior year abroad at the University of Bordeaux, reading a Céline novel was still suspect.

III

Under the spell of a Drycleaner lecture detailing the polemics between Céline and Jean-Paul Sartre—who had accused Céline after the war of having been *paid* to spout Nazi theses—I wandered into the Museum of the Resistance, down the block from the Bordeaux *gendarmerie*. I told the librarian I had started studying the author of *Bagatelles pour un massacre*: what could she tell me about him?

She led me from the front desk into a room in back of an exhibition space where she kept her files. She raised her voice. "How can you work on a collaborationist when we have so many fine resistance writers to offer—Aragon, Triolet, Vercors—each of them so lyrical, so inspiring! A young person like you shouldn't be thinking about this fascist!"

I emphasized that I wasn't in favor of fascists; my father had prosecuted Nazis at Nuremberg. It was important for me to know why writers had gone wrong, especially a good one like Céline.

Her voice softened immediately. The line about my father worked. Except I was lying. I had made myself out to be a literary prosecutor, my interest in Céline "official." That was only part of what drew me to Céline. The rest had to do with what happened while I was reading him, the music I felt in my heart, a sense of lightness and magic, as well as a total confidence in this writer's knowledge of the depths of individual human suffering. Our literature professor wanted us to hear that music; the Resistance museum official was implying that people who celebrated Céline's prose style were whitewashing an evil man of all responsibility for his language.

Barbara's sobriquet for our teacher—the Drycleaner—was more appropriate than we knew.

IV

Irreconcilable positions like the museum official's and the Drycleaner's stances on Céline made the writer even more appealing to me. I read him in college and in graduate school. It wasn't until I started teaching, after my Ph.D., that my French was good enough to work on his postwar novels, webs of historical allusion so complex I needed an annotated edition to follow them. I found music and tenderness and delicacy in the postwar Céline, too. His sentences got shorter, his rhythms bebop; he made his reader more and more present, closer and closer to the scene, such as this moonlit Allied bombardment from *Rigadoon*, the last book Céline wrote:

> Je me dis: Lili, je te retrouve, t'es là! . . . Bébert aussi! . . . oh, mais les sirènes . . . que de sirènes! . . . autant qu'à Berlin . . . ici ils devraient avoir fini, assez ratatiné tout! . . . enfin, à peu près . . . ou alors! . . . uuuh! . . . alerte encore . . . d'un bout du clair de lune à l'autre . . . j'oubliais de vous dire, il faisait un de ces clairs de lune!
> . . . uuuh! . . . brang! . . . braoum! . . . des bombes . . . des bombes, oui! . . . elles pouvaient écraser quoi? tiens, et Felipe? . . .

I tell myself: Lili, I've found you, you're here! . . . Bébert too! . . . oh, but the sirens . . . nothing but sirens . . . as many as in Berlin . . . they should be done around here, they've wrecked everything! . . . or pretty nearly . . . uhh-oh! . . . uurrh! . . . another alert . . . from one end of the *clair de lune* to the next . . . I forgot to tell you, it was one of those incredible moonlit nights! . . . uurrh!! whamm! . . . vroomm! . . . bombs . . . more bombs, yes . . . what's there to smash? hey, where's Felipe?

I'm right there with him, waiting for a bomb to drop on my head. I hear him, I light a match in the dark with his words; I see the flash of moonlight on three scared people and a cat scrambling in the dark, breathing hard, listening for each other: Céline, Lili, Felipe, and Bébert the cat.

When I finally heard Céline's voice on a tape recording I was shocked; what I had imagined from passages like this one from *Rigadoon* was a lilting poet. His "real" spoken voice was raspy and croaking, broken.

How could somebody so bitter, so broken, make light and magic and music on the page? If he could transform his hideous voice into music, think of what I could do.

Céline made me want to write.

I'm not alone in this reaction. Since Henry Miller, Americans have been drawn to the mixture of spleen and fantasy in Céline and have tried to get something of his rhythm and emotional directness into their own prose. Even Jewish writers, women writers, have been able to bracket the biographical fact of his racist diatribes and his misogynist lust and humor: Philip Roth claims Céline as his Proust ("I feel called by his voice"); Vivian Gornick prefers his "radiant poison" to Miller and Mailer's more everyday misogyny.

In addition to these appealing writers who have spoken out for Céline, there is one man whose relationship to Céline has appalled and fascinated me: Milton Hindus. I've identified with him, completely; I've disdained him; I've wanted nothing more than to be *unlike* him in my scholarly relationship to Céline. Like me, he was a literature professor, a Jew; like me, he wanted to write after reading Céline. For years I refused to read Hindus's book on Céline, *The Crippled Giant*, because Céline scholars I talked to in France said it was "moralizing psychology, American style"—I certainly didn't want to do any of *that!* I quickly leafed through Céline's letters to Hindus, published as an appendix to *The Crippled Giant*. The two men had corresponded while Céline was in exile in Denmark. Hindus, a young professor at the University of Chicago, had signed a petition with other American intellectuals arguing that Céline was guilty of unpopular opinions—not political collaboration—and that the Danes shouldn't extradite him to France. The petition worked and Céline answered Hindus's first letter in a spirit of genuine gratitude.

My research on Céline's influence on American writers took me to Carlton Lake's collection of correspondence and manuscripts at the Ransom Center in Austin, Texas. I had gone to study Céline's letters to his American editors at Little Brown. As an afterthought I ordered the complete Hindus-Céline archive (including the original Céline letters, in French, and typed copies of Hindus's English-language responses). Once I began reading both sides of the famous correspondence, unedited, I was hooked.

Hindus sent Céline coffee and tea by the poundful from Macy's, financed by the advances from James Laughlin, publisher of New Directions, on reissues of Céline's work. Hindus called Céline his master; Céline called Hindus an angel. Hindus sent questions about contemporary literary figures: Morand, Aymé, Claudel in France; Dreiser, Hemingway, Sinclair Lewis in the U.S. Céline obliged with page upon page of reflection about literature that have since become the cornerstone for all studies of his art. I sympathized both with the young professor wanting to please and profit from his literary mentor and with the ravaged exile, isolated, fearing for his life, seeking contact with a more innocent world—and absolution through friendship with a Jewish intellectual who adored him.

In the course of their correspondence, Hindus encouraged Céline to articulate his ideas about literature, most famously the notion that to make writing sound like the spoken voice, you have to distort language, much the way you have to bend a stick to get it to look straight in a glass of water. Bend it, but not too much!

Hindus had gotten Céline to reveal the complexity of his thinking about art. What Hindus himself had to say, as far as I was concerned, was secondary—he was handmaiden to Céline's genius.

As I read both sides of the correspondence, I was overwhelmed by the image of a dutiful tortoise straining to keep up with a hare. Céline sends Hindus one funny, brilliant, ribald letter after another; Hindus looks for ways to match his master. The U.S. publication of the Kinsey Report spurs Hindus into an attempt at bawdiness. He confesses a voyeuristic dream to Céline, in which window shades are pulled up to reveal human licentiousness (he's vague, even when he's trying to be scandalous, so that we aren't sure what the actual licentiousness is). His dream reminds him of one of his favorite scenes in *Voyage*. Aren't all real novelists voyeurs, he asks, wishfully? He risks a reference to homosexual voyeurism in Proust. In a postscript, he requests that Céline not show his letter to Madame Céline; such talk must remain between men.

Hindus is making love to Céline—or trying.

In 1948, Hindus travelled to Denmark to visit his pen pal in person. Hindus was shocked by Céline's appearance, habits, moods. The powerful writer drooled, harping monotonously on the same themes; he showed no interest in the kind of civilized literary dialogue Hindus had fantasized. Céline was impatient and irritable with a guest who, instead of sparring back, became more and more awkward, fussy, annoying.

Each French critic who has told the story of Milton Hindus's trip to see Céline is obliged to point out the American professor's naivete, his academic rigidity, his lack of imagination and charm: the American was incapable of understanding a "real" writer! Many recount scenes where Céline and his wife, Lucette Almasour, greet Hindus in the nude in front of their Danish hut—nudity, they add with ethnographic precision, being a normal aspect of Danish life that skittish Hindus, the American puritan, couldn't take.

When I first read those stories I thought—"I would never have behaved that way around Céline!" It was a ridiculous thought, because in 1948, as a woman, I probably wouldn't have had a Ph.D., would never have been considered for a teaching job at the University of Chicago, would never have traveled to Denmark to interview him. But my mind wouldn't quit trying to identify with Hindus. Today when I reread the same passages in the biographies, I'm still indignant at the ethnocentrism of the French: why do you have to paint all Americans as naive and prudish? Why do you think we can't appreciate the depths of your world, your nakedness? Why do you have to make Milton Hindus a scapegoat for the utter failure of Céline—your failure—to face the dark places in your own history?

Hindus returned to Chicago in September 1948, "burned," he said in a last letter he sent to Céline on the continent, by the force of Céline's personality. The two men kept up the pretense of correspondence for another year.

There's a box in the Ransom Library in Texas marked "uncatalogued," containing the correspondence between Céline and Hindus in 1949, after Hindus has returned to America. The final exchange between the two men is as vivid to me as though it happened yesterday—the speed and energy with which I switch my sympathy from one correspondent to the next makes me suspect I've found two parts of my own personality in these letters—two feuding parts. Here's how I reconstruct the story around Céline and Hindus's final exchange:

Agonizing over his visit, still fascinated, Hindus begins to draft a literary essay on Céline; his working title is *The Monstrous Giant*. Now, at last, *he's* the writer. He puts down on the page his most passionate thoughts about literature, the product of graduate school and teaching the Great Books at the University of Chicago, linking all his insights to the universal themes in the works of Louis-Ferdinand Céline. He poses the problem of Céline's work and Céline's personality. He narrates the voyage to Denmark—his first trip to Europe. He speculates about Céline's power, madness, and human shortcomings.

Since returning to the U.S., Hindus has switched jobs from the University of Chicago to Brandeis. Working in the first Jewish-sponsored university in the United States, with a Jewish-identified faculty and staff, his choice to work on the most infamous anti-Semitic writer in Europe in the aftermath of the Holocaust is conspicuous, to say the least. Hindus struggles in his mind to justify himself. He does so in the name of literature.

On January 12, 1949, Hindus tells Céline about his new job at Brandeis, enclosing a clipping from *Look* magazine, making a boyish remark about the pretty girls featured in the photo illustrations. He signs off by cheerfully reporting that he has gotten a lot of spleen off his chest by writing about his trip; it's made him feel better to write about it. Would Céline please read it? He must promise not to be offended.

(The article in *Look* is a public relations fluff piece about Brandeis, illustrated with pictures of college girls at play.)

Grotesque, Hindus! You are so fatuous, two-faced—you're anything but naive, which is what the French accuse you of being. You are insidious, provocative. Why are you sending a guilt- and paranoia-crazed anti-Semite an article about Brandeis University? You're playing him like an instrument; seeing what the evocation of long-legged Jewish girls doing ballet exercises is going to do to the polemicist whose most violent racist work, *Bagatelles pour un massacre*, consisted of responses to Jewish newspapers, Jewish theater groups, Jewish politicians.

It's the equivalent of giving crack to an addict.

Céline writes back to Hindus on January 20, maintaining

his charming banter: what a perfect job it would be for his wife, Lucette (a dancer), to teach dance at Brandeis! But please, Hindus, don't sent me your travel writing—send coffee instead!

January 29. Hindus dutifully promises coffee, insists that his sketch of Céline isn't really so bad. If only his friend Céline were with him at Brandeis—the place is so utterly lacking in wit.

Why is Hindus telling Céline he wishes he were at Brandeis? Is he idiotic, or subtly sadistic? What is going on in your head, Hindus?

February 10. The remark about "wit" sends Céline over the edge. Sour, suspicious, provoked by the disingenuous promise Hindus wants to exact from him not to be offended by his sketch, Céline lobs back a Célinian grenade. What's wrong with those Jews at Brandeis? Céline asks. The girls have great thighs (he's looking at *Look*)—it's a compensation. He'd like to be there himself, really he would. What a good joke: he'd make himself out to be a Nazi to really turn them on. They'd be in the clouds, those Brandeis girls, getting screwed by a Nazi, even an old one. He'd pant into their ears—"Just like in Buchenwald."

There is nothing in the archives to tell us what Hindus felt in February 1949 when he read Céline's letter.

I had read Céline's February 10 letter first. It made my stomach turn, my insides curdle. This is what language can do; this is evil! I read Hindus's January 12 and January 29 letters hours later: "You asked for it, you jerk," was my first response. You provoked it. You sent Céline the words you knew would make him respond as only Céline could respond. You elicited his worst hate language—you wanted the proof, all over again, of how hateful he was.

VI

Céline was emotionally accurate in his cruelty. He knew just where to hit when he struck back at Hindus. Babbitt plus Judas, he later called him, in October 1949. A weakling in search of literary glory at any cost. Hindus only liked novels that were tailor-made for professors of stenography.

Céline read the manuscript that Hindus sent him, finally entitled *The Crippled Giant*. Céline's reaction was due not only to the fact that he could dish out insults, but not take them; he was genuinely panicked, convinced that Hindus's analysis would prejudice his legal defense in France. The way Céline saw it, any criticism at so delicate a moment could be a death sentence.

Céline fought Hindus the way he knew best, with words. He threatened a libel suit. He organized friends to write Hindus. He even wrote to the president of Brandeis University in an outraged bourgeois tone (he could turn it on like a faucet), accusing young Professor Hindus of indecent behavior toward the ladies (!), cretinism, lying, being a bore, and not knowing a word of French. "He does not even know the difference between "le mauvais goût" and "un mauvais goût."

While his letters to and about Hindus grew nasty and threatening, Céline's correspondence with Jean Paulhan, the representative of his powerful new French publisher, the Editions Gallimard, was sweetening. Céline complains about foreigners' bad taste in a gesture of literary bonding with his fellow countryman: "They can only understand Rolland, Romains, Gide—model Berlitz guides. The foreigners want *dead French* that doesn't disturb them." When I read these sentences, I wanted to argue with Céline, play the foreigner to his Frenchman. He's dead wrong about foreigners—at least about this one. I *want* to be disturbed by a foreign language; I want French that's alive. Before Céline, I knew French for buying groceries and doing well in school. I was hollow in French, André told me so. I got hooked on Céline because he was the farthest from official French I could get in a book. There are thousands of American readers and writers like me; Céline himself, whether out of self-hate, xenophobia, or ignorance, had us all pegged as fools.

Céline was wrong, specifically, about Hindus. He thought Hindus's *Crippled Giant* would prejudice his trial. Instead, the book (published in New York in 1950, in Paris in 1951) brought Céline to the attention of postwar readers in France and the United States. Placing Céline in a pantheon of "great writers," it separated Céline the literary genius from the unpleasant person and anti-Semitic polemicist. Readers could read Céline comfortably, without feeling complicity with World War II genocide.

Hindus was the first in a long, distinguished line of Célinian drycleaners.

VII

The University of Paris VII, built after the student revolts of 1968, feels like a high security prison. Inside a small office lined with notebooks containing Céline's press clippings, the wind howls past leaky windows. French graduate students, ambitious and expert young men with cigarette-stained fingers, are working at two long seminar tables. The date is June 1986. I'm examining a page of Céline's first and longest racist tome, *Bagatelles pour un massacre*, with Professor Godard, who is advising me on my research.

I stop at a word I don't recognize: "gode." Céline has changed André Gide's name to "André Gode."

"André Gode?" I say, out loud.

"Do you know what it means?" one of the students pipes up, lifting his chin from his own papers and eying me like a game show host.

"Yes, of course."

I had no idea what "gode" meant; I wasn't going to admit it, not at Paris VII, not among Célinians. I assumed it was obscene.

The glossary to Céline's complete works listed "gode," the noun, "object imitating a man's sexual organ" and "goder" the verb, "to reach orgasm or simply have pleasure." It turns out to be one of Céline's favorite words.

The student was blushing, but there was an "it's mine not yours" look in his eyes along with the embarrassment. I narrowed my gaze at him to see if I could get him to blush even more. It worked.

I'm supposed to be the American prude à la Hindus, I thought happily, only this guy is much more uncomfortable than I am.

"Rest your voice," Professor Godard said as I was leaving the office, "you'll need it tomorrow for the colloquium."

I headed from Paris VII to meet Monique, a French friend from graduate school who had promised to listen to my lecture and check for mistakes. Rachael, a fellow graduate student and my summer roommate in Paris, met us at Monique's apartment on the rue Monge. Rachael teased me about getting so worked up over a bunch of Céline specialists. "Those people are nuts—half of them are reactionaries, the others think they're Simon Wiesenthal! Only the linguists are sane, and they don't talk about what interests you!"

"But you'll help me, won't you?"

I had twenty minutes to present all I knew about the cheap anti-Semitic leaflets Céline had scavenged to write *Bagatelles pour un massacre*. The research had taken me three years.

Rachael and Monique timed me to the minute and took notes.

"It's fine, really," Monique concluded, "except you're pronouncing all the words beginning in 'is' or ending in 'isme' with a 'z' sound instead of an 's' sound."

In the 1930s, Jewish refugees from Hitler had spoken French this way, substituting "z"s for "s"s. It was a mistake Céline would have loved to imitate in his depiction of the foreign hoards who were weakening France. The specific words I was mispronouncing—"communisme," "fascisme," "anti-semitisme," and "israélite"—weren't random. They were the key words for any debate about Céline.

My phonetic unconscious was hard at work.

VIII

The 1986 Céline colloquium began early in the morning in a large Paris VII auditorium. After the first speech, people started yelling at each other: "Are you suggesting that Céline was fascist!" "You call that evidence!" "I will not accept ignorance in the place of argument!" I was scared. More was at stake than at the American conferences I was used to.

A man came up to me at the morning coffee break and said that if I gave him a copy of my paper he'd footnote me in his important book on Céline's politics, currently in galley proofs. He'd make a special effort to include me.

I gripped my briefcase until my knuckles were white.

When my time came at the podium I pronounced "issraélite," "fascissme," "communissme" according to Monique's coaching. The unnatural composure I get making speeches had come over me; I looked at my audience calmly, measuring my pace and intonation:

> Beaucoup des questions que nous nous posons sur la composition de Bagatelles pour un massacre et les forces culturelles qui ont façonné celui-ci trouvent leur réponse dans les pages de ce livre. Car c'est dans Bagatelles que Céline a commencé à utiliser systématiquement le trait narratif qui devait devenir le label de ses chroniques d'après-guerre: trait que Godard appelle "un discours en train de se faire" et qui se caractérise par de constantes références de la part de Céline à son contexte quotidien . . . à des textes que le narrateur affirme avoir lus à l'instant, et qui semblent être l'aiguillon qui l'a incité à écrire. . . .

We can find a response to many of the questions that have been raised about the composition of Bagatelles pour un massacre and the cultural forces that shaped it, right in the pages of the book. In Bagatelles, Céline inaugurated the systematic use of a narrative technique that was to become the trademark of his postwar novels—a technique Godard has called "discourse in the making," which we can characterize by the constant references on Céline's part to his immediate daily context . . . to texts the narrator claims to have read at that very instant, provoking him to write. . . .

Halfway through my talk, Milton Hindus's face came looming into my head—or rather not the Hindus face itself, which I had never seen—but the image Céline had given it:

An iceberg with glasses.

My plan for the lecture had been to be icy-dry and scholarly. I didn't want any interpretation in my analysis, only
facts. I would be "scientific" (in French the adjective "scien-
tifique" is often applied to literary research); I would be beyond reproach. It had to be perfect, or they were going to
attack me the way they attacked Hindus, who let his
personality—his weakness—show in his book on Céline.

A postcard I picked up in Texas the week I spent with the
Hindus-Céline correspondence convinced me that I was
closer that June 1986 morning to being a Texas armadillo
than an iceberg: "This burrowing mammal is covered with a
bony shell. When attacked, the armadillo may roll up like a
ball and depend upon its own armor for protection." When
I read the Hindus-Céline correspondence, six years after
making my scientific speech, I understood that not wanting
to be Hindus—not wanting to show my horror and desire
for Céline—had made me a latter-day Hindus, cool and re-
pressed. I also understood that my disdain for Hindus's
project—for his "Americanness"—made me a latter-day
Célinian xenophobe.

I love Céline for language and emotional directness I
don't have. But in the end—I always want to put a "but" at
the beginning of every sentence I write about him—he was
paranoid; his reactions distorted the harsh realities he
sensed so acutely, but couldn't tolerate. He didn't see that
Hindus was helping him by painting him as a great flawed
writer. He never understood that Hindus's portrait of him,
Hindus's publication of their literary correspondence, did
as much to "pardon" him for future generations of readers
as the amnesty given to one Dr. Destouches by an absent-
minded French magistrate.

Hindus, for his part, was phony in his letters to Céline, trying to please him with silly regrets that Europe's most infamous anti-Semite wasn't a professor at Brandeis. He was two-faced as well, because at the same time he was inviting Céline to Brandeis, he was devastating the Céline personality in his own writing. Writing in the most passionate "literary" style he could muster, he was competing with Céline, the way critics invariably compete with the writers they're supposed to be analyzing.

The French critics have always taken Hindus for a masochist, a Jewish critic willing to take the greater writer's verbal abuse. What they don't acknowledge as easily is the power Hindus exercised as Céline's only Jewish friend, the thrill, for a thirty-two-year-old American professor, of rescuing a writer in trouble, then putting him under a microscope.

What's Céline to me? When I was nineteen, a college student, I wanted his musical slang; I emulated his exile. When I was thirty-two, a professor—the age of Milton Hindus when he left for Denmark—I wanted to catalog his every anti-Semitic quotation with scientific precision. I am thirty-eight, and Céline is still with me: it's his anger I envy most today, his anger and his directness.

Hindus is the person in me who wants to please, who wants to get it right, who can't say when he's angry, what he wants—or admit his power when he has it.

Hindus is the good student, the placater. Céline is the reaction to platitudes, fakery, injustice; the counterattack.

After a week in Texas with the Céline-Hindus letters, I felt I understood the two men; if pressed I could have kept the correspondence going, playing each role wholeheartedly.

Part Four: *Revisions*

In Search of the French "R"

My students often call me "Madame." Especially in the South, where "Madame" is such an easy slide from "Ma'am." Not Ms., not Professor, not Dr., but "Madame," without a surname, in that sweet serious way they learn in grade-school French class. When I hear myself called "Madame," I become the shopkeeper, the governess, the secretary, the schoolteacher, trained in body and voice to serve. I am a Parisian woman in a white smock, standing behind her pastries or her scarves or her fountain pens, patiently waiting for my customer to decide. I am the teacher of my first fifth-grade French class at Northrop School in 1965. My fifteen students rise in their blue uniforms. They say "Bonjour Madame" in unison when I enter the room.

"Madame, Madame," I hear the cry for help from the back of the room. "Comment dit-on 'doorknob' en français?"

When I hear "Madame" I am not an intellectual. I am part mother, part policeman, part dictionary.

"Poignet de porte . . ." (I'm pleased that I know it)

"mais je ne suis pas dictionnaire!" (professional responsibility: I'm not a dictionary).

"La prochaine fois, cherchez le mot vous-même." (Next time, look it up yourself.)

The first French teacher I ever called Madame was Madame Holmgren, her looks emphatically French, her name inexplicably Norwegian. She was a tired dowdy woman with very black hair, beige clothes, and an almost sickly pale skin punctuated by a mole. Thinking back, I imagine that she must have been a war bride supplementing a husband's slender income and putting her daughter through private school. Her daughter, Christine, was in our class. Christine was dressed as though she had been born a hundred years before the rest of us. Her hair was combed severely and kept out of her face with an oversized tortoise shell pin. She had round owl glasses with black frames. Her uniform blouse had a round Peter Pan collar, rather than the square kind that we wore. The top button of her blouse was buttoned tight, hiding her neck. Her mother's body was an object of extreme fascination because of the hair on her legs—dark whiskery hair, the first hair any of us had ever seen on a grown woman's legs. Did we speculate on the hair under her arms or did we see it when the weather turned hot, and the dresses sleeveless? Did we imagine that she never used deodorant because a grownup told us that the French were supposed to smell, or did we decide she didn't smell the same as we did? We talked about Madame Holmgren behind her back. It was 1965; the United States had barely closed its military bases in France. France was still a defeated, shabby, foreign place. We associated Madame Holmgren with the unknown excretions of a womanhood that we were on the verge of experiencing in our own bodies. Was it Nurse Nelson, our hygiene teacher, who told us that THERE ARE NO TAMPAX IN FRANCE?

Poor Madame Holmgren, not knowing all we had said about her, had to teach us the names of French body parts from a blue book about the Famille Vincent. The class dissolved into titters over Le Bras, with its arrow pointing to Mme Vincent's arm. For us the word wasn't about arms, it was a bra, a brassiere, more bra-like for that embarrassingly sexual "r" we were supposed to put in our throats saying it. Making the "r" meant moving your tongue around and feeling the vibrations in your throat. That was mortifying. "Bras" with its sticky sound was just one more part of the foreign sensorium already represented by the legs, underarms, and odors of Madame H. We refused to say the word and refused her an explanation of our refusal beyond our giggles. To this day I hesitate when I write "bras," still tempted to spell it without an "s."

In my school you weren't supposed to try too hard. You were supposed to be good at things without lifting a finger. Good at sports, an effortless fling of stick and the field hockey puck sailed halfway down the field. Good in class, capable of a sarcastic retort but never too involved in the argument. A-minus on the quiz without studying. Who would want to wrench their mouth out of shape to make a French "r" or a "u"? It would be like admitting you kissed boys, or wanted to. Or that you looked yourself over in the mirror when nobody was looking. Trying too hard meant not belonging, not being really smart.

We wore uniforms—navy jumpers with button-down powder-blue shirts underneath (preferably Gant or Brooks Brothers, with loops in back.) If you slouched just the right way you could make the jumper loose enough above the waist to stick your hands in through the sides, as though it were a muff.

Most of the time I was in line, part of the great majority who didn't want to make an ass of herself. An R Resister. I could speak in long strings of words ending in "ya know?" without ever really opening my mouth—this in spite of buck teeth and braces. I could laugh with an inward snort, like a pig, or with an outward "heehee," by blowing the air through my teeth. My language was slouched, in a studied kind of way, like my jumper. I could listen without appearing to listen, speak without appearing to speak. My vernacular skills were refined; why should I change shapes?

On the other hand, I knew what it was supposed to sound like. I heard Holmgren's "r." And I knew that by comparison our resistant "r" was a flat, closed-off smashed version of the truer sound. So let's say I did decide to risk it, make it ok, this foreign "r," I still had a dilemma: the American "r" sounded stupid, Midwestern, but to get the French one right I knew there would be an awkward apprenticeship where it would come out all slobbery and wrong. Like kissing a boy with braces on.

How to do it? Where to do it? Will my braces stick to his? Will they pry us apart with pliers?

Won't everybody laugh?

If I hadn't gone to Switzerland I would have stayed stuck. If it hadn't been for Frichot, his smile with the glint, his approval, disapproval. I liked to look up at my teachers and see them smile. I became a teacher because I wanted the chance to give the smile, or withhold it. There is nothing cruder, nothing simpler, in terms of pedagogic power than what goes on in a language classroom: listening, repeating, listening, spurred on by the sound and rhythm of someone else's voice, by mockery and desire for revenge.

The language classroom is bare-bones pedagogy, the rawest pedagogical situation I have ever been in. A place where content means almost nothing and power, desire, provocation almost everything.

I like the story about a French critic who came up against one of those perpetual language students who was only interested in the sound of French and wasn't afraid to admit it. The critic had just delivered a lecture, in French, on the writer Georges Bataille. It was a complicated argument: a theory of the avant-garde (including a definition of modernism), quotations from Bataille's little-known anthropological writings, and a whole new perspective on the 1930s. A single hand was raised in the question-and-answer period: "Sir," an American asked in her best French, "aren't you speaking in the accent of Marseilles?"

Learning languages can show up people's craziness in dramatic ways.

I had a student who ate constantly in class. It was summer school, an intensive course, long consecutive hours of work. I finally put my foot down when she brought in a chicken. An entire chicken cut into pieces—she'd slip a piece out of her bag every fifteen minutes or so and gnaw on it ferociously. She spoke with meat and bones in her mouth, a latter-day Demosthenes. Every time I introduced a new vocabulary word, she started chewing on another joint. No one could concentrate, the smell of chicken overwhelmed us, the sound of crunching bone competed with our exercises. It was my mouth against hers: I had to forbid this R Resister even the smallest snack.

The famous stories I know about language learning are in this genre, battles of the will with fierce parental overtones. The polyglot writer Elias Canetti describes his mother teaching him German by holding the book away from him, throwing her hands over her head when he got it wrong and shouting "My son's an idiot! I didn't realize that my son's an idiot!" And Louis Wolfson, a mental patient from New York who lived with his mother, has written a whole book in a stiff, self-taught French about learning languages in his mother's house as a way of negating her presence. Then there is the case of Freud and Breuer's patient Anna O, the brilliant young German woman who insisted on speaking English to her doctors and nurses, and who, like a teacher, got them to speak English back. Speaking about her treatment in the language that was foreign to her, Anna O invented one of the great catch phrases of psychoanalysis: *the talking cure.*

Talking cures: like analysts, language teachers are always in search of the foolproof method that will work for any living language and will make people perfectly at home in their acquired tongue.

I was told the story of language teaching when I was learning to become a teacher. Once upon a time, the story goes, all languages were taught like Greek and Latin. Learning was based on grammar rules and translation. You talked in your own language about the dead language you saw written down. Then in the late nineteenth century came the Direct Method, the ancestor of Berlitz. You spoke in class in the language you were trying to teach; you worked on pronunciation; you practiced grammar out loud.

Pearl Harbor gave the first big boost to the teaching of modern languages in the United States. Linguists developed practical and efficient methods for the soldiers and spies going off to Europe. From the forties on, people looked to linguistics to revolutionize language teaching: language classrooms would be "labs" with scientific data and results; the emphasis would be on speaking, speaking like natives and learning like native speakers do. In the late 1950s, Noam Chomsky argued that children acquire language more or less automatically by the time they are five and whatever makes it happen can't be duplicated by adults—it has nothing to do with situation. Chomsky's insight did language teachers absolutely no good: they couldn't duplicate genetic processes, and they couldn't hope to reproduce childhood as a model for second-language learning.

A second historical boost to American language teaching came with the Soviet launch of Sputnik into space. American fear about being behind the Russians in math, science, physics, and foreign languages fueled a National Defense Education Act, which promoted a method based on the memorization of set dialogues in foreign languages, called ALM (Audio-Lingual Method). ALM didn't last long: it came under fire for its Skinnerian behaviorism, its dependence on rote memorization, its dry and arbitrary content. Its critics began to called it "planned parrothood" because, although it gave teachers total control, it created students who could do nothing but mimic.

Language teaching methods make for a tale of enthusiasm and skepticism, hope and hope dashed. Every once in a while someone comes along and promises a new language method, like Rassias at Dartmouth. Rassias instructors snap their fingers in class to keep the words coming quick and even, like Beatniks, and I've heard it said that instructors will go as far as to crack eggs on students' heads, just to keep their juices flowing. ALM with new props? Still no perfect method in sight.

Whatever the method, only desire can make a student learn a language, desire and necessity. This is why some immigrants learn language so well—they have to. In a classroom, you can make the language student feel "just off the boat." The method is called "immersion" (sink or swim), and it works very well. But even with immersion—especially with immersion—you need more than language, you need to represent the culture that the second language lets you in on.

The latest hope of language teachers involves abandoning drills in favor of what they call "communication in context." Put flesh on the bare bones of pedagogy, they say; if you can create a viable fictional world in which language students can participate, their second language will have both use and meaning.

The first day I went in the classroom to teach French, I was a nervous wreck. The lesson was about saying hello. These were my instructions: the teacher is a moving target, maintaining a constant flow of correct French. I was supposed to say hello to each student in a variety of French ways, shake hands, get them to say hello back. I was supposed to move around the room and keep moving, so the students' eyes would keep darting after me. I was so sure that my French was incorrect that I asked Béatrice Abetti, the assistant at the language lab, to go out to lunch with me beforehand and listen to me in French and assure me that I could teach. I was remembering Madame Holmgren and how mean we were about her—racist, it suddenly dawned on me as I thought about it, in my sophisticated graduate student way. Too late: now I was Madame Holmgren, human loudspeaker, my body up front, the living breathing example.

I was trained to teach according to the Capretz method, in the "sink or swim" tradition. Every week Pierre Capretz would present an episode in the ongoing story of Robert and Mireille, and we, the new teachers, would spend the subsequent week assimilating it with our class. No English is spoken, ever. There are no exercises in translation. When I taught it, the Capretz method existed only in the form of mimeographed booklets and weekly multimedia shows in the Yale language lab. It has now been expensively produced in video format, on location, using professional actors; it has been broadcast several times on educational TV. Some of my friends have the Capretz tapes on their VCR. Like Fonda exercises you can use to get your French in shape.

The story is the usual light romance: Robert, an American student, goes to France to study at the Sorbonne and meets Mireille, a Parisian. The grammar is woven into the plot. The week we study families is also the week we study possessive pronouns: my uncle, your father, her sister. As for the story itself, we can reinvent it, recombine the elements, make the plot turn new ways. I ask the class, "What if Mireille hadn't walked out onto the street at that moment, would she have met Robert?" "No, she wouldn't have met him": presto, they're practicing the past conditional and the placement of the direct object pronoun. I put them in dialogue with one another: one is Robert, calling Mireille on the phone. Then the reverse. The class loves making the sounds that aren't language: sirens, telephones, French ducks that say "quin quin" instead of "quack." Students start dressing like Robert and Mireille, talking like them, anticipating their every move.

The Capretz method reproduces the conditions by which a student on her junior year abroad might learn French language and culture, by hearing the constant flow of correct French and by being in situations in French, complete with background noise and the emotional dilemmas that come from the push and pull of everyday conversation. On a Capretz test, students will listen to a loudspeaker announcement in a department store over the din of the shoppers, and will have to make it out. Or they'll have to decipher the words to a song, or one-liners in a stand-up comic's routine. Unlike immigrants, for whom these situations are traumatic, the students can practice the scenes over and over again in class. The student situations are vaudeville romantic. No one is unemployed or hungry. No one will flunk a citizenship test or be sent back to Ellis Island.

This method always appealed to me. It corresponds to what I liked best about being in France: being-in-situation with language, every new event and personality in life a chance to try something out. Only with the method it's a story, not real life. And I, Madame, control it, I set the game working: I'm the school driver, the one who picks them up at the airport and shows them the way home.

Teaching, I discover, is not really about my French, my body, and whether or not they're correct. It's about generating words—other people's words. Making people change, making them make mistakes, making them care and not care, making them sensitive, but not oversensitive, to the nuances of language. Making them take risks. It is physical, shockingly physical. Not just because I am there, walking across the room so their eyes won't fall asleep, but because I, Madame, have to make their mouths work. I walk up to a student and I take her mouth in my hand; I arrange it in the shape of a perfect O. Too close, a little too close to repeat.

Occasionally I divide our bodies in half, our left side speaking English, our right side speaking French so we can feel the difference in our posture, our hands, our muscles. Our English side slouches, while our French side is crisp and pointed. In English we gesture downwards with one hand, in French our entire arm is in a constant upward movement. With our French side, we shake imaginary dirt from our hand with a repeated flick of the wrist, to show we are impressed, scandalized, amused. This is interesting, to be double like this with them, and funny enough for comfort. Also from Capretz I learn to teach tricks that no one ever taught me for making French sounds. For the "r," gargling with mouthwash to feel the vibration in your throat. This tells you where the French "r" is, until finally you can do it without the aid. Making the "u" sound—the "u" in "tu" or "fondu" or "bu," that most French of French sounds—is a three-part pedagogy. First you say "o" with your mouth in a perfect round (as though you were going to peck someone on the check), then "eee" (with your mouth stretched out in a horizontal smile like a trout, or a wide pumpkin), then a combination of the two: with your mouth in the shape of a perfect "o," you say "ee." The sound "u" comes out. This works well.

The Capretz method depends on students not making things up, it teaches them to absorb and recycle ready-made bits of language. It asks them to listen to the tapes in the lab and let the story of the week sink in, like a hit song that you listen to in the car on your way into work and end up knowing in spite of yourself. This is hard. American students want A's for originality. They can't believe that language isn't theirs to remake. They compensate with theatricality: by the end of a good semester a Capretz class is a repertory theater; the students, method actors. The extroverts learn French so well by this method that it frightens me.

This is what teaching is like, too, knowing that you are teaching better than you yourself ever learned, that you can get more from your students than you were ever capable of giving. Teaching, if it succeeds, is dealing with the fact that some of those hams will be better than you are.

"French wasn't like this for me," I murmur to myself as I am teaching this miraculous Capretz method, "it was more private, whispered." I remember the first poem I learned, Victor Hugo's autumn poem, full of low hisses:

L'aube est moins claire, l'air moins chaud, le ciel moins pur;
Les longs jours sont passés, les mois charmants finissent.
Hélas! voici déjà les arbres qui jaunissent! . . .
L'automne est triste avec sa bise et son brouillard,
Et l'été qui s'enfuit est un ami qui part.

The sunrise is less clear, the air less hot, the sky less pure;
The long days are past; the charming months finish.
Alas! Here already, the trees that yellow! . . .
Autumn is sad with its north wind and its fog,
And the summer that flees is a friend who leaves.

The poem is simple, and beautiful mostly for its sounds: a hissing of the north wind in the "s"s, just enough to blow some leaves off the trees. A "u" sound hidden in the last line. And the "ar" sound in the last word, "part," it has a nice sliding away sound to me. My mouth feels good when I say it. I'm not tired of it, even though I once listened to two hundred students recite it for one of those Alliance Française events where the local high school students come to the university to "declaim" Hugo and Baudelaire. I feel religious about it, because of having known it before I knew what it meant.

My friends in public school who had the Audio-Lingual Method dialogues could all recite the same scene they didn't understand—about a tailor, I think. At my girls' school we had Mauger's *Cours de langue et de civilisation française à l'usage des étrangers*, a series of blue books put out by the Alliance Française, the worldwide organization that promotes French language and civilization. In the introduction to my copy of Mauger, copyrighted 1953, French is described as a language for the elites, useful and beautiful: "French uplifts and it serves." The Mauger story follows the Canadian Vincent family as they embark on a visit to see their friends the Legrands in France. They take a boat—a *paquebot*. Their friend is a bookseller, has a maid who serves dinner. They eat frequently in Paris—12:30 in a restaurant; tea at 4; dinner at home at 7:45.

It's unfair to complain that people in language books are eating too much; it takes a few meals, at least, to show the difference between a definite and an indefinite article. (I would like the pie versus I would like some pie). Besides which, everyone eats, and not everyone lays bricks, operates printing presses, or looks at amoebae under microscopes. Everyone needs the words for food.

It amuses me that I now know the extraneous words, the minor details in the black and white drawings of French rooms in the Mauger book. What social class is being represented. What neighborhood in Paris they might live in. I recognize the Henri IV dining room set, the *traversin* pillow across the bed. I know that French intellectuals, French executives prefer to work at desks with no drawers like the one in the Legrands' study. The places where the food is sold are places I have been—disappearing now, of course—the butcher shops where the rabbits hang with their fur and the sausages look like necklaces. The grammar tables in the back of the book, too, are inscribed in my mind like so many separate boutiques: the er verbs, then the ir verbs, the verbs conjugated in the past with "être" instead of "avoir." It took forever to acquire these details, a whole adulthood, it seems, and I'm not done. Time enough for the France they inhabit to be gone: Mauger's grammar looks as dated to me now as those fifties Robert Doisneau photographs, where the French men wear berets and frayed overcoats in their postwar leanness. It's a France as old as pissoirs and segregated-sex lycées and women just getting the vote. France before Les Halles was torn down. France without a single fast food, France still hungry.

A different kind of landmark: in 1966 I first heard the word "existentialism." I was at the Vanderveers' house, and Priscilla's brother, a senior in high school, was writing a paper for his seminar in Great Ideas. It was the longest word I had ever heard. French was this, too, always—even in beginning French classes you knew there was a France beyond the everyday, a France of hard talk and intellect, where God was dead and you were on your own, totally responsible.

In the summer of 1968 I went to French camp in Bar Harbor, Maine, and read Camus's *The Stranger* for the first of many times. At camp there was a rule that if you were caught speaking a word of English you would get a "mauvais point," a black mark. For every *mauvais point* you would have to memorize a certain number of verses of French poetry before you were allowed to go into town. I don't remember the poetry (Baudelaire, probably) but I have an exact memory of the lobster I ate when I was released from recitation. Once I was caught speaking English with a nightgown over my head—I slipped the nightgown down and there was the monitrice, pencil in hand, grinning.

Why grinning? Why are these language teachers always grinning, glinting, mocking? There is something sadistic about language teaching that works. You assume the authority, and along with it, the sadism. You give or withhold the smile.

Language teaching is badly paid, little recognized, and much maligned. It is left up to native speakers for whom it is stupidly thought to be "natural," therefore too easy to be of much value. Ph.D.'s want to move on from language teaching to the teaching of literature, and theories of literature. Language teaching is too elemental, too bare. You burn out, generating all that excitement about repetition, creating trust, listening, always listening. In literature class you can lean back in the seat and let the book speak for itself. In language class you are constantly moving, chasing after sound.

When I think back on Capretz's method, in this light, I remember some of the cartoons he would show for comic relief. Bodies coming apart. Patients on the operating table. Black humor. Humor teaches better than sincerity—violent humor. It's violent being thrown into a new language and having to make your way. Violent and vulnerable: in a new language, you are unbuttoned, opened up.

In 1990 a group of Yale undergraduates filed a complaint with a sexual harassment grievance board against "French in Action"—the Capretz video method—claiming its sexism was preventing them from learning the language. They pointed out that the camera focused far too often on women in skimpy T-shirts; that men were the action figures in the stories, while women were either sexy objects of contemplation or fat and frumpy objects of ridicule. In the most contested episode of the video series, the female character

Mireille is sitting in the Luxembourg Gardens reading a book when the pick-up artist Jean-Pierre comes along and tries to get her to talk by making comments about her skirt. She resists by refusing to say a word. A language course teaching women's silence?

Yale student Jacqueline Shafer, in her reaction to this and other scenes, wrote: "At times I felt I was enrolled in a class aimed at titillating and encouraging male students who might otherwise not be interested in learning French, while the women were expected to ignore and/or overcome their own discomfort with the images before them—women, in other words, were supposed to take care of themselves. Like the women Jean-Pierre harasses, I was expected to step aside."

I taught those scenes from 1978 to 1981. I joked, with the other French instructors trained in the Capretz method, that we were perpetuating a sexist bourgeois world view— but I was only joking. When the Yale students filed their complaint in 1991, I admired their action—but I couldn't join them wholeheartedly. I analyzed the debate, I recognized the flaws, but I didn't condemn "French in Action." I had gotten too much from it.

"It was not what France gave you but what it did not take away from you that was important": Gertrude Stein published that line in *Paris France* in 1940, the year her adopted country caved in to the Nazis.

I've been willing to overlook in French culture what I wouldn't accept in my own, for the privilege of living in translation.

Learning French and learning to think, learning to desire, is all mixed up in my head, until I can't tell the difference. French is what released me from the cool complacency of the R Resisters, made me want, and like wanting, unbuttoned me and sent me packing. French demands my obedience, gives me permission to try too hard, to squinch up my face to make the words sound right. French houses words like "existentialism" that connote abstract thinking, difficulties to which I can get the key. And body parts which I can claim. French got me away from my family and taught me how to talk. Made me an adult. And the whole drama of it is in that "r," how deep in my throat, how different it feels.

Tenses

The difference between the *passé composé* and the *imparfait* is something every French teacher learns to teach, one of the standard rites of the pedagogy. You learn to draw a time line. You go up to the blackboard, and it's dramatic, and you say, "this is the imperfect: the imperfect is for description; it's for events that haven't finished." The time it takes to say this is just about the time it takes to drag your chalk line, slowly, all the way across the board. You pick up your chalk and you explain, chalk in hand, that the imperfect is used to describe feelings, states of being; it's used to describe background, landscape, and ongoing thoughts. All sorts of things with no definite beginning and end. Then you pause, take hold of your chalk piece like a weapon, and you stab that blackboard line at one point, then at another. This is the *passé composé*, this staccato: a point on the imperfect line of experience, a discrete action in the past with a beginning and an end that you can name.

I was walking to the parking lot [unfinished action] when I tripped [sudden discrete action].

It was nice out that day [description: *il faisait beau*], so we went [narrative event] to the park.

Even Grevisse's venerable *Bon Usage* (Good Usage—the standard French grammar manual) refers to the imperfect as a "process line." Life has description and life has plot. The French divide it up in such a way that you always know what tense to use. The air was still as glass when the tornado touched down. Was—*imparfait*; touched—*passé composé*.

For a French professor there is no way to talk about tenses without remembering Camus's *The Stranger*. It's the linchpin in courses, joining grammar and literature, the first novel in French that American students read. *The Stranger* is supposed to favor the *passé composé* over the *imparfait*: critics argue about this. The story is supposed to be, in some philosophical sense, about the difference between the two.

The story: a white guy, a petty bureaucrat in a French company in Algiers, kills an Arab on the beach. He is tried for murder. Testimony reveals that he went to a Fernandel movie the day after his mother's funeral (Fernandel was a famous comic actor), and to the beach. About the murder he claims, when pressed, that the heat of the sun made him do it. He is the Stranger. He is condemned, his head to be cut off in a public square in the name of the French people.

The man's life begins as he realizes he's about to die. Happiness as he watches the sun rise and fall in the slit in his cell. He can just see the water, just see the beach. In his cell, about to be guillotined for the murder of an Arab on a sunny day, the Stranger writes: "I think that I slept because I woke with stars on my face. I felt ready to relive everything." I felt: "je me suis senti" (*passé composé*) and not the expected, "je me sentais" (*imparfait*). Feelings are usually supposed to be in the imperfect. The whole point of the book, the point that this nuance of tense expresses all by itself, is that nothing in the Stranger's life lasts long enough to be written in the imperfect. He is in prison, and he is going to die. Life for the Stranger is existentialist: here we learn the big word, even though it's not a word that Camus himself would have used in 1942 when he wrote *The Stranger*. We also learn that "Stranger" can mean foreigner—like us, learning French— or it can mean, in a purely psychological sense, an alien or outsider. In the novel the narrator is both: he is a foreigner in Algeria, a colonial bureaucrat, and he is estranged from ordinary language. He can't muster up the conventionality to tell his girlfriend that he loves her, or cry at his mother's funeral.

The tools I had for understanding the story weren't sociological ones, they were the tenses and the conditionals. I didn't know that Algeria was a colony. That the Stranger wasn't a foreigner but a colonizer, a *petit colonisateur* working in an office. I didn't understand how shocking it was that when the Stranger's boss asked him if he wanted to go work in the Paris office, the Stranger didn't jump for joy. This was, for the French reader, the ultimate sign of a man lacking all normal ambition. No ongoing desires. It is macabre that most American students learn French from this story of freedom achieved through the murder of an Arab. The Arab himself is usually considered incidental. *We*, the readers, are the strangers to French. The Stranger outdoes us, he is a stranger to our conventional lives, with his desires that come and go in a minute, his indifference to planning, to eating, to marriage. Desire, for him, is no more than a stimulus response:

J'ai senti ses jambes autour des miennes et je l'ai désirée.

I felt her legs around mine and I desired her.

and, in prison, talking to himself in the *passé composé*, the Stranger claims:

Je n'ai jamais eu de véritable imagination.

I never had any real imagination.

This we were taught to admire. That denial of imagination was part of the aura that existential literature gave out. It was marked by the constant awareness of death and indifference to context—beach or cell. We cut our teeth on it, then we learned to teach the murder of an Arab. Discuss whether the sun made him do it, or what it means that he says so. Philosophical claims: there may be no tomorrow, experience is fleeting, feelings are strangers to one's self. And literary claims: sentences come and go, too, with no connections between them. The *Stranger* was our inauguration to the world of description and truth, an inauguration in which history—the history of the Meursaults of Algeria, the history of the nameless dead Arab, the history of the author Camus, a poor boy who made it from Algiers to Paris by virtue of his seamless sentences—was never mentioned.

In our advanced courses, much later, comes the possibility for a total shift in tone, a past for events that are so long gone they are wrapped in the shrouds of time: "il fut un temps" [there was a time] is the French equivalent of "once upon a time." This distant tense, called the *passé simple* or *passé historique* signals a past that is beyond our reach, the past of legend:

Louis XVI fut exécuté le 21 janvier 1793, place de la Révolution,
aujourd'hui place de la Concorde.

Louis XVI was executed the 21st of January, 1793, on
what was then the Place de la Révolution, today Place de
la Concorde.

TV announcers use the *passé simple*. Professors use it. Students use it as a joke when they want to sound pretentious.

I used to get emotional about tenses when I taught grammar. I'd invent personalities for each tense. The *passé composé* was easy—that was Meursault's tense, one time only in the past, easy come easy go. The *imparfait* was just that—imperfect—it captured those indefinite, unsatisfied human conditions. The subjunctive: most of life takes place in the subjunctive, not the indicative—one action subjecting, subjugating itself in the subordinate clause to a realm of feeling or doubt. "I am afraid [feeling] that you don't understand [subjunctive]" versus "I know [certainty] that you understand [indicative]."

The subjunctive has a schoolyard reputation for extreme formality since it's the last verb form people learn in the grammar sequence—second year. I remember my feelings of expertise when I could rattle off my tongue, "Il va falloir que je m'en aille" (I'm going to have to go now), and glide out of a room. The subjunctive is really something else; realm of doubt, desire, fear and trembling before language.

I think about the tenses all the time, especially that slash in the imperfect time line, proving that a sudden event can come and disturb the smooth thoughtlessness of everyday living. The time line is my theory of history; my own history fits it to a tee.

Guy, de Man, and Me

I

William Golden's father was an American businessman in the garment district, Seventh Avenue; his fortunes rose and fell with hemlines. Periodically he would show up in New Haven and stay in his son's apartment for weeks at a time, doing the dishes and hanging out at Naples Pizza. William's mother was an ex-mannequin from Paris, rich now and living in Neuilly with a second husband and French preppie children; she was indifferent to the son who reminded her of a tacky first marriage. She had fled New York when William was five, leaving him with his father. The father sent William to the Lycée Français de New York, partly out of nostalgia for the mother, partly for the tuition break. The lycée, heavily subsidized by the French government, costs much less than the average New York private school.

The split between his school language and his home language did its work on William from an early age. French came to represent the absent mother—aesthetically imperious, demanding, rejecting; after-school English the unsupervised, blasé, frequently unemployed New York Dad.

William had two distinct personae. A French *moi*, exceedingly fastidious, clean of diction, light of step. We used to call him, in translation, Guillaume Doré. Guy for short. Guy was thin, exceedingly so, and his French self was neat to a fault. "Tip top" [pronounced "teep tup"] is the English phrase that the French use to describe such impeccable self-presentation. Cardigans, flannel pants, the left hand posed in the air to mark a particular stage in Cartesian dialectic. William's other was American *me*, "Bill," who slouched, knew baseball statistics from the sixties, listened to reggae, drank from cans at the graduate student bar, ate beer nuts, and played poker.

These personae were in limited contact with one another. I would have been better off having the relationship with Bill. I met Bill at the Gypsy Bar; Guillaume on the first day of Peter Brooks's Balzac class. Bill liked me. But it was Guillaume Doré I wanted and Guillaume Doré I got.

He had come to Yale graduate school fresh from his college thesis on existentialism. He was obsessed with Sartre and with bad faith and—of all things for someone totally out of contact with his other half—with authenticity. Paul de Man's course in theory drove the existentialism out of him pretty fast, but substituted deconstruction, which was even less forgiving. Because there wasn't even a person there to be inauthentic—deconstruction was about keeping person-ness away. Later I decided that Guillaume chose de Man as his mentor because de Man, like Guillaume's absent mother, was impossible to please. De Man didn't even believe in pedagogy! So how could Guillaume learn his lessons?

At the literature lectures everyone on the faculty watched de Man's face, to gauge his reaction. The question asked by de Man was the center of gravity of any intellectual event. During my first year in graduate school, a young don came from Oxbridge to lecture on Mallarmé. De Man sat in his usual third row seat, his head sunk into his tweed jacket like a turtle's. After the talk, at the precise moment when de Man's head emerged from his collar and he lifted his hand and twinkled his eye, the don went ramrod stiff, whipped out his pencil and held it to his paper in nervous alert. All before de Man had uttered the first word of his question. At the time it seemed to me the reversal of what should go on at a lecture—shouldn't the lecturer be telling de Man something and not the other way around? It was embarrassing.

Guy and I were in de Man's "Introduction to Literary Theory." It was for first- and second-year students only. The class met in a windowless seminar room in Cross Campus Library, an undergraduate library that had been built underground, beneath the quad. Afterwards a bunch of us would gather in Machine City, a lounge set behind the walkway leading from Cross Campus to the venerable old Sterling Library. We'd settle in a small formica booth, drink bad coffee and eat Lorna Doones from the vending machine as we tried to fathom what had gone on in class. The big question was, "What is deconstruction?" Guy had the surest answer, "deconstruction is when you figure out that a story or a poem is in the wrong—not because the author is lying, but because there is something inherently deceitful about language. Language can never tell the whole truth. It's the deconstructive critic's job to find the places where language breaks down, by looking up close and finding language's sleight of hand."

De Man was working on the rhetorical figure known as "catechresis" (I kept thinking about it in my mind as "catechism"). It was the key to the whole way we students tried to think about language. A figure of speech is usually a substitute for the "real" "proper" meaning. Metaphor, for example, means "jumping over" the basic meaning of a word to get to the poetic meaning. When you call dawn "rosy fingered," you're making the sun into a hand and its rays into fingers. Metonymy works with another kind of substitution: you identify a person or thing by some part of them, you call the man with red hair "Red." Metonymy is the figure of selection and desire: you nickname your friend after the part of them that you like and notice most. But sometimes substitutions break down. Certain words don't have a meaning of their own; they borrow their meaning from another realm. Like "leaf" for a page of a book (from the world of trees) or "leg" for a table (from the human body). "Table leg" and "book leaf" are both instances of "catechresis." With catechresis, the substitute figure (leg, borrowed from the human anatomy; leaf, borrowed from nature) is the only word available: there is no proper meaning underneath, no foundation for the figure, no literal meaning. That was a deconstructive insight.

In the class, I wrote down de Man's examples, and even his asides; the key to the mystery might be anywhere. The man who began to look like his dog (an example of metonymy); how he taught for Berlitz when he first came to this country; jokes about marriage. The concept of "mise en abîme" was a big deal. De Man explained "mise en abîme" by describing a cocoa can with a girl on it holding a cocoa can with a girl on it holding a cocoa can. When does it stop? There are problems, concluded de Man, with trying to represent reality.

The first step in any systematic literary analysis, de Man taught us, was to chart the polarities, the systems of oppositions in the language of a text. For a metaphor to function, it has to be convincing. Shades of Proust: "the duchess's eye, blue like a ray of sun." A sun looking over the world—like an eye. The image involves an inside, an outside, nature and art, hot and cold. How can a ray of sun be cold and blue?

At the heart of this question was another, simple and basic, that de Man had extracted from the rhetorical logic of literary language. Metaphor needed to convince by sensual means, and one metaphor had a way of engendering another, until you could find a whole set of transformations that made up the solidity of the text, the recognizability of style or author. A sun can't be cold and blue unless it turns away from itself, as an eye, a glance, can turn away from anything—except itself. Why, de Man asked us, are blindness and insight such powerful combinations? Because the sun makes it possible for us to see, but if we look at the sun too hard, we go blind. Oedipus saw the truth about his mother and father, and he went blind. Too much light is blinding.

Too much light is blinding; too much knowledge is ignorance: the polarities were swimming around in my brain on the day a student walked out of class. He was a very formal person, an older student who wore a three-piece suit and carried a Cross pen-and-pencil set. He stood up and read a paragraph to the class from the assignment for the day, an article by Gérard Genette called "La Métonymie chez Proust" (metonymy in Proust). "I don't understand this paragraph. And, furthermore, I don't think it's capable of being understood." That's the way he talked. And then he left.

It was a clincher: by leaving, he made the rest of us feel like survivors. We were the ones who stayed, we were banking on our ability to understand. But sometimes I think about him, and I think that he was a hero. He knew what he wanted and wasn't afraid to say it. He wanted to understand—what was so bad about that? He had more courage than the rest of us, pretending we understood when we didn't.

Understanding, de Man intoned, was only a metaphor borrowed from the physical world. To understand is to "stand under," to support. To put up with something! Most of the vocabulary of knowledge was borrowed from the physical realm, he reminded us, from the world of sight (now I see) or the world of eating (I'm digesting an argument).

The weirdest part of the episode with the student was that de Man didn't mind his departure. He was more sympathetic towards the departing student than he was towards those of us who stayed. He wouldn't let us scorn the deserter. He didn't think that deconstructive theory could be taught or even understood. He pointed out that every human being had a limited amount of reading time in life and that we ought to decide what we wanted to spend it on. Reading a single sentence by the French philosopher Jacques Derrida could take hours. We had to figure out if we'd rather spend it on a novel. We could probably get through Proust's entire *Remembrance of Things Past* in the time it took to read Derrida's *Grammatology*.

This was how de Man undercut his own authority. Or like this: after a student made a comment, he muttered "bien"— well done. As soon as he said it, he got that wistful smile on his face and he apologized, saying how much he hated the set-up where the student waits for the teacher to say "bien," like a dog waiting for a bone. When I first thought about it I felt grateful to him for refusing to manipulate us but later I got mad: the way he told it, we were just eager dogs, needy and vulnerable. Did he think we would scrounge for any scrap?

When our first paper was due he told us, out of the blue, that anyone who could come up with an *original* paper would get "Honors" (we were graded "Pass," "High Pass," or "Honors"). Originality? We had never heard about originality from de Man before. What could originality mean when reading itself was well nigh impossible? Of course people blocked on the paper—every idea seemed so obvious. Or else they slavishly tried to do exactly what they thought de Man would do: the disinterested close analysis.

That year de Man and a couple of his colleagues published a book of essays called *Deconstruction and Criticism*. Suddenly it was named, it was a school, and we were in it and liable to be asked to explain it at dinner parties. Roger Shattuck, a critic in Virginia, wrote an angry article in the *New York Review of Books* saying that we, graduate students at Yale, were a bunch of anti-humanists, inferior to our learned teachers. We were deluding ourselves with the crazy fantasy that we could be like social scientists with foolproof methods. What we should be doing, Shattuck said, was reading poetry out loud and feeling its beauty. We had lost touch with literature.

But Shattuck was wrong. No one had ever paid more attention to literature than de Man did. We responded to him because of his ability to trim away anything that wasn't literature—he was the only literary critic we had ever encountered who seemed to know exactly what he was studying.

When de Man's students went in to see him he had to remind them to think about practical matters—what was the right topic for the market, who should be on their committee, who could write them a grant letter—because none of them ever talked about that. They talked about literature.

The establishment critics (the adults out there) hated

him, because he was indifferent to so much of what had come to pass for criticism: evocation of context; celebration of great ideas; appreciation of what was beautiful. De Man wanted to know what literature was; and unlike most critics, he was willing to take the next step and see where what he knew broke down, where literature made a fool of his attempt to understand it. That's what put the twinkle in his eye, that final step of undoing—that was his originality and the source of his power.

Rachael, who came to graduate school from California my second year, described the essence of deconstruction as "hunkering down over a text": the way de Man could take a perfectly ordinary paragraph and make it contain all the mysteries of language and knowledge. There was a religious quality to the reading he inspired. Rachael's boyfriend in Boston liked to get stoned with his friends and take turns reading from de Man's "The Rhetoric of Temporality" out loud . . . just to feel how hard and mysterious the words were.

I remember the feeling of reading a de Man article. The beginning was lucid, too lucid. He would go on for five, ten, fifteen pages. It was literary history, chronology, as plain and reassuring as can be. He would start with a cliché of romanticism, a received idea about allegory, a distinction—allegory versus symbol, or metonymy versus metaphor—the kind of distinction that critics rely upon to do their job. He showed how much he knew, casually.

Thrilling, this first part, because you knew it was a mask. The world, the text, weren't transparent. Enjoy being lulled because the mask is going to come off.

In the first fifteen pages of the article would come the Passage from the Text. In de Man articles the quotation that was going to serve as the kernel for a deconstructive reading was big, it was generous, a text that you could get your teeth into. Being a critic meant reading: the article really started here. You would read through the passage six or seven times to see if you could anticipate the blind spot he was going to find. Like reading through a hospital mortality report to see if you could figure out what the patient died from before you got to the end.

My memory of the body of de Man's text gets hazy, right here where the important part begins. The point in the article where he zeros in on the blind spot. It usually has to do with rhetoric, with the promise of the rhetorical figure to be just that, with its failure to be *only* that. With its manipulativeness, its unexpected something elseness. There's always a trick at work. The critic has to show why a metaphor is believable, and how it transforms what it describes. De Man used Hitchcock's film *North by Northwest* to explain the power of metaphor. He talked about the moment in the film when Cary Grant kisses a girl in a train compartment, and the camera switches to a shot of a train going into a tunnel. The train going into a tunnel was a metaphor, because foreplay, in a heterosexual world, leads to penetration. It seems natural to show a train going through a tunnel because the two main characters are seated in a train, but it's also a metaphor for sex. This all happens in the split second of a film frame, just as metaphor happens in the split second of one word substituted for another. The substitution is so fast you hardly know what's going on. When you think of it, you laugh.

As we got closer and closer to writing our term papers, Guy lost interest in sex. "La femme est toujours en rut" ("woman is always in heat"): he quoted Baudelaire at me accusingly when I sidled up to him on our walk home from class. He couldn't spend the night. He had a paper to write on metaphor.

We tried studying together at Guy's apartment. Bolstered by his Random House dictionary, his Old French dictionary, his Petit Robert Dictionary, he was reading, quoting, scrutinizing, while I raced through my assignments, impatient, hungry for plot, hungry for dinner, too, and a little human contact. When Guy went to the kitchen to get us a sandwich I snuck a look at one of his papers from the medieval French seminar he had taken first year, a course he never talked about. It was sitting on his desk as though he wanted me to see it with comments all over it. The comments were dithyrambic, the professor practically begging him to turn the paper into a full-fledged dissertation, detailed philological study, words and their history. But Guy was attracted to the big stuff, Meaning, not meanings. He didn't value what he was good at.

Guy came to my house to study next. He made a crack about how few books I had, and I thought, What the fuck am I doing here? I had sold all my textbooks when I was an undergraduate, in California. I wasn't an intellectual. Intellectuals don't sell their books back to the bookstore.

We were getting down to the wire. I couldn't concentrate on reading for as long as Guy could. I didn't recognize the names of literary characters alluded to in the criticism; the examples of rhetorical figures and narrative devices were from books I hadn't read. I didn't know half the authors being talked about: German philosophers from the nineteenth century in addition to the whole canon of French basics that I had skipped over in college to get to the contemporary work. I had cut corners in classes all semester, not reading through to the end. I hadn't had any training in philosophy. Often it seemed like I had been following the changes in the professors' tones of voice, more than what they were saying. "That last part was the punch line," I would think, not knowing what it meant. I wondered if I was really a survivor.

Guy had set himself a military schedule for writing his metaphor paper. I was supposed to be writing on metonymy, the trope of desire, in the works of Benjamin Constant. I called Guy on Friday night and told him I had to see him. He came over, annoyed. He didn't want to spend much time, five or ten minutes. I demanded he stay the night. I clung to his sleeve; he yelled; I yelled louder; he stiffened up; I grabbed harder. He slapped me across the face. Hard.

I had never seen Guy look scared.

"I've never hit anyone," he said. He tiptoed out of the house.

I don't know what it was like for Guy to finish his papers that semester. I know I was relieved to be alone. There was no expert eye over my shoulder, no thicker book across my desk, no rigorous schedule making me look lazy. Suddenly I wasn't lazy anymore. I could work for hours without noticing the time. I wondered—in that secret part of my brain where I admitted my responsibility—if I hadn't provoked Guy into hitting me.

Guy and I got back on speaking terms ten months later. It was the beginning of my second year at Yale, his third year. He walked into the Commons lunchroom behind a woman with a huge bandage on her hand. They joined me. She was a first-year student in French from California. She had burned her hand lighting the gas stove in her apartment on Bradley Street, down the street from Guy. Guy had gotten her to the doctor. He was "rescuing" another first-year student.

Unlike me, Rachael wasn't hooked by Guy. She already had a boyfriend, a writer in Boston who was halfway through a first novel based on the childhood of Jimmy Hoffa. Rachael wasn't obsessed with French, either. She liked avant-garde writers, Beckett and Blanchot in France and Burroughs and Wallace Stevens at home. She liked theories, the wilder the better: Norman O. Brown's polymorphous perversity, Gilles Deleuze's schizo-desire. She liked pinball machines and grilled cheese sandwiches. Rachael, Guy, and I ate lunch together in the Commons every week. Rachael could do a perfect imitation of Professor Harold Bloom saying "Oh my dears, oh my dears." Together we made up names for our professors and fellow students: "the yachtsman"; "le beau ténébreux." She had a story about each of them. Together we invented a character named Irving, our academic valet. "Irving is writing me a footnote on the Hegelian notion of the relève." "Will you ask Irving what metalepsis is?" Being with Rachael made the world look like a comic strip—an American comic strip. William and I went into a new phase of our competition—we vied for Rachael's friendship.

I resolved to go ahead with a dissertation on French fascist writers. I had never really stopped thinking about them since I discovered Céline as an undergraduate. I chose Dan as my adviser—a Malraux scholar. He lived down the street, and walking home from school one day, I asked him to direct my dissertation. He invited me into his house for a beer to celebrate. He knew the left critique of fascism inside out, but he hadn't read the fascist intellectuals; he asked me about pronouns in their writing and whether there were questions of style I could focus on. I'd get exasperated talking to him because I had my own idea of what I wanted to do and he would make it more complicated, or more straightforward. I felt vengeful about working on fascist intellectuals—intellectual life isn't really so high-minded; look at the trouble these people got themselves into. French people! As much as I loved France, I was dying to find the country's blemishes, her crimes. I also thought that deconstructionist theory could get me further in my dissertation. Maybe I could have it both ways—I could deconstruct fascism, and I could show that intellectuals were just as subject as anyone else to fascist longings. Derrida had talked about the primacy of voice in Western philosophy, so that's where I began, with descriptions of voice in novels and essays written by writers who were enthused about fascism.

I read books that weren't in print anymore: Robert Brasillach on the Nuremberg rallies, Drieu la Rochelle's perverse theories of French depopulation, Marinetti's Franco-Italian futurist manifesto, avant-garde artists pulling themselves out of the maternal ditch, soaring along in their sports cars through the modern city. The French fascists loved the energy of the futurists. The hardest writer to describe politically was Céline, experimental in his style, reactionary in his ideas. He could say the worst drivel and make you laugh; his political position was racist and reactionary but anti-authoritarian at the same time—like one of those right-wing populists on call-in radio.

I had been taught, as part of the deconstructionist climate, that it was more interesting to think in terms of rhetorical structure than historical periods, and I had chosen to work on material that made history impossible to ignore. France had fallen in six weeks in 1940; the country had been occupied by the Germans, but the French themselves had formed a government at Vichy with its home-grown enthusiasm for anti-Semitic nationalism. The books I was reading were all wrapped up in position-taking; some of the fascist writers were so far gone in their enthusiasm for Hitler that they considered the Vichy proponents old-fashioned and ineffectual. They had their sights set on the new Europe. Meanwhile, I knew so little about the history that I had to look up most of the proper names in dictionaries. I was sure that no one in New Haven had ever read the books I was reading; they weren't "literary." Whatever value they had was in showing what it sounded like for an intellectual to endorse European fascism. I was dying to show how screwed-up intellectuals could get about the truth. Here was my chance to transgress a purity that I mistrusted in literary studies. I loved thinking about France in crisis, France where politics ruled literature, where censors shaped editions, where writers were out of control with hate and prejudice.

Other motors were fueling my interest in the thesis, and they had nothing to do with school. There was my imaginary conversation with my father about punishing war criminals. In his last year of life, my father had read Hannah Arendt on the Eichmann trials. I tried to get into his head by reading it. I fixed on the phrase that Arendt had used to describe the horrors of the Nazi mentality, the phrase I wanted to ask him about: "The Banality of Evil." How could so many people—soldiers and bureaucrats but also intellectuals and poets—be blind to so much horror?

Dan reminded me of what everyone at Yale knew: that de Man's uncle, Henri de Man, had been an important socialist in Belgium and had signed a collaboration pact with the Nazis in 1940. By coming to the United States, de Man had freed himself from an embarrassing episode of family history. I imagined the disinterested rhetorician, cleansed of his family's historical improprieties. The pure intellectual had found his true home in the American University, where parties and politics didn't matter. Clearly he would have thought it was bizarre that I wanted to stick my nose in so much bad thinking. I never went to talk to him about my thesis.

Dan read my drafts right away. At first he was grouchy—I was sloppy, I couldn't spell, my English was awkward from reading too much French—but as I got going, he started distinguishing what was clear from what was turgid, and even though he hadn't read any of the texts I was working on, he could tell when my arguments were too slight.

I was writing about fascism and desire. Crowds, wanting to be part of the Motherland, following the voice of a leader. The themes were coming together—I had been so hesitant a student, and now, at the dissertation phase, was the sea change. I was a "late bloomer." I knew what I wanted to write; I was writing in my own voice.

Dan read my pages faster and faster as I went on; after six months he said, "this is good." "C'est bien!" I didn't feel like a dog scrounging for a bone, I felt great.

*　*　*

In the fall of 1979 I went to look for jobs for the first time. You applied by putting together a dossier of letters of recommendation at the Career Center, answering ads in the Modern Language Association job list, and waiting for your dossier to be ordered in the hope that the next step would be an interview at the MLA convention, which took place at the worst possible time of year—the three days after Christmas. The first year was a bust for me—I wrote fifty letters and five schools ordered my dossier, but no one asked me for an interview. I speculated with Dan that a dissertation on fascism looked like I must be a fascist—you didn't work on literature you didn't admire. As part of his concern about my job prospects, Dan started to take a proprietary interest in my person. He didn't like my hair, which I had just cut short to the scalp and spiky. "No one will hire you looking like that. You look scary."

"You sexist dog," I said, "you only like women with long hair." We were getting along pretty well.

The next fall Dan was denied tenure. He hadn't gotten the one or two interesting jobs at the senior level that had come on the market, and he didn't want to teach at a crummy school. He decided he would rather go to law school.

I went on the job market for another round. This year Dan went to check on my dossier before it went out. He found a letter with a sentence in it that read, "her French didn't used to be very good." "Right," he said when he told me about it—"your French was terrible when you were in kindergarten." As soon as he removed the letter with the slur, I started getting interviews. One of the schools that called me said I was the first "Yalie" they'd been able to interview in three years. They couldn't understand dissertation titles like "Catechresis and the Impossibility of Reference"—much less the dissertations. They had a hundred undergraduate French majors, half of whom spent their junior year in France, and they wanted these students to know something about the place—books and ideas, that sort of thing. The anti-deconstruction backlash was in gear; I was going to benefit from it.

The week before I finished the thesis I went to Dan's to work on the rough draft of my conclusion. He said, "I want to go to bed with you." Just like that.

"Oh, come on!" His wife and son weren't home. I can tell you what I was wearing that day—a blue plaid skirt and a white T-shirt, and I was freckled and strong from jogging with William and Rachael. I sat on the couch in his living room, and I gave him a little lecture about why he thought he wanted to sleep with me:

"You're leaving literature and I'm your last connection to literature, and you're powerful with me, so of course it's symbolic and you're wanting to hang on, via me."

He grinned. "Your writing is sexy," he said. "Reading your writing makes me want to sleep with you."

"My writing? Come on!"

Of course, I wanted to sleep with him. I felt electric and powerful—my writing *was* sexy, desire passed through it. Of course, I didn't want to sleep with him. I was too close to being done, I needed to concentrate. How dare he risk my degree for a lark?

"You're out of your mind," I said.

"No, I'm not," he said. Neither of us ever mentioned it again.

We jogged our way through the last six months in New Haven, Rachael, William, and I. We jogged together and listened to the news. Synagogues were being bombed in France and fascism didn't seem so far removed. We ran six miles each day, past the reservoir, to the Hamden movie theater, and back to the corner of Lawrence and Orange Street. If I wasn't relaxed, I'd go to the Yale gym and swim another mile. I was taking a job in an unknown state where I didn't want to go, but I was lucky to have a job. The women in literature met in the sauna at the gym and made nervous conversation about jobs. We worried. I kept going to get my clothes taken in at Rosie the tailor's, and when Rosie told me I was getting too thin, I felt like I was back in Switzerland.

When I finished the thesis, I turned it over to a committee of four readers and waited for the reports to come back. One of them was Fredric Jameson, a Marxist critic who was writing a book about an English modernist with fascist sympathies named Wyndham Lewis. I used to brave the lines of bearded Marxists outside his door, and he had rewarded me with bibliography and encouragement all along. He liked the thesis. There was an older guy, who had been in Paris in the thirties, and he liked it. And an Italian, who thought I was moralistic, but liked it. Dan was proud: "It's important for you that Jameson likes it" (Jameson was another world, not deconstruction, but another legitimate way of reading); "I knew he'd like it. Damn it, I knew it was good."

My dissertation passed through the department, although Dan said that there was an argument in the faculty meeting. "Why would she want to work on those horrible writers?" There was some debate about whether I should get a prize. They hemmed and hawed and finally decided no, "because it wasn't literature." Dan was angry with them; I told him I didn't need a prize. Their argument was my prize.

Dan left for law school that summer, in California; Guy

and I left for our jobs. Yale was still placing students, although the market for Ph.D.'s was terrible. One school advertised for an instructor who would teach five courses a semester of French, Spanish, and piano—for $14,000 a year! Guy took a job at a big state university in the northwest; I headed south to another state school. Rachael went to California with a job in comparative literature. Guy and I had to teach first-year French to students who didn't want to be there but had to be, because it was a requirement. I went home every night and read the want ads—just to know that there were jobs in the world other than the one I had. I saw French mistakes I had never even dreamed of—letters that didn't exist, words that bore no relation to any language. I graded and wept.

Guy had written his dissertation on irony, irony in Gérard de Nerval. It was like pulling teeth: a year of work on a single poem, trying to get logical inconsistencies in each metaphor. He came home from his job every day with that five-hundred-page deconstruction of Gérard de Nerval lying on his desk like an affront. One Monday morning he walked up to the blackboard to conjugate, looked around at a sea of students in tractor caps, and that was the end.

Rachael called to tell me about it. She had the story directly from Guy. "He walked!" The department chair had even called him at his father's place in Rochester and begged him to stay—they liked him so much—and he said he was never going back.

Rachael and I were on the phone every week our first year out of Yale, keeping each other going. The Guy story was one of our favorites.

"Ph.D.'s driving cabs all over the country and he just up and resigned a tenure-track position!" she said.

"I can't believe it," I said. But I could believe it.

None of us was prepared to deal with the difference between our training and our actual work, teaching French.

II

De Man died in 1984, of a cancer that had moved very fast. We heard stories of people at the hospital bed, jotting down the last words—a cult till the end. De Man himself was flawlessly brave, showing interest in his illness as though it were someone else's. I cried when I got the news—cried for the death of my student life, more than for the distant teacher.

I had spent two years teaching language at the state school, then three tough years at Columbia, a "revolving door" position with no job security but opportunity for career advancement. It worked—I finally landed my dream job at Duke, where I could teach twentieth-century literature to undergraduate and graduate students, and where I got tenure.

Guy went into a retraining program for Ph.D.'s. It turned out he had a genius for technical writing—he could now cultivate that sense of philological detail he had tried to ignore in graduate school. Around this time he met a woman and fell in love and got married. She understood about Guillaume Doré, I think, but she loved and rooted for Bill. Both of them had had difficult family lives, and a series of unhappy relationships, and now they had found their main chance. The former deconstructionist was going to have kids and a house and a garden—the whole picture, no apologies. When I saw them in upstate New York one summer, he was beaming. And wearing overalls. I remembered how de Man had said to us in class, "don't confuse any of this literary theory with your lives"—how we hadn't believed him, how we had wanted our criticism to tell us how to think and how to speak and how to live. De Man made literature matter more than anything in the world and then said it was only literature. He had put us all in a bind.

III

The year Bill Golden fell in love and married, word trickled back from a conference in Alabama: a Belgian graduate student had discovered that de Man, our de Man, had written literary and political columns for a collaborationist Belgian newspaper during the war. A job he got from his uncle. Some of the articles were pro-Nazi; one was anti-Semitic. Our teacher had been a collaborator.

There was ugly scandal-mongering in the newspapers. Everyone who had ever competed with de Man, who had ever resented his success, came out of the woodwork with their statement. His first wife implied he was a bigamist. He had come to New York after the war and started life anew, hung around with the *Partisan Review* crowd in New York, taught at Bennington and married the daughter of a U.S. Senator, who smoothed the way for his new visa. Various people claimed they had known all along. The de Manians said: "This is a non-event; the revelation is a pure rhetorical construction, perpetrated by the media."

But de Man had written that if French Jewish novelists were sent to a Jewish colony, the literary life of Europe wouldn't suffer. That sentence had been lying around in the old-newspaper room; now it was in photocopies on the desk of every literary theorist in the country.

The people who were most attached to deconstruction were the most vociferous about how inferior, stupid, unreliable, vulgar, and irresponsible was the journalism being written about the de Man scandal.

You could smell the disdain on one side and the glee on the other.

As for me, I was finally going to get that long overdue "Honors" for originality. I was a literary critic who had been at Yale in the heyday of deconstructionist criticism, who had studied collaborationist intellectuals of the 1930s and 1940s in de Man's department. I knew the books de Man had reviewed at *Le Soir*, the Belgian newspaper he had worked at, because they were the books I read for my dissertation. I knew the people he referred to in the books. If I didn't, I knew how to find out who they were. I knew exactly what to do. I waxed tragic but I had an adrenaline rush that lasted for months. I got the bound volumes of *Le Soir*, with de Man's articles in them. Under his by-line was every fascist cliché, every inane argument I had catalogued about the New Europe: one month, a glowing reference to futurism as the poetry of the New Europe; the next, a joke about Céline. There were distinctions within the collaborationist rhetoric that showed he was discerning, even as he was toeing the line; there was a review of Brasillach, calling him a softie who confused politics with art. I crouched on the floor of my office with yellow legal pads and breathed in the dust and in two months wrote an article that ordinarily would have taken me a year. I put all my erudition to work, with a vengeance. Suddenly this dissertation work, this topic that had seemed completely irrelevant to literary theory circa 1978, was relevant. Every deconstructionist in the country wanted to know what fascism was, and I was in a position to tell them. None of these theorists had ever thought that the political history of France in World War II was worth a damn for thinking about literature; let them work at it now, I thought, let them look up all the proper names and the political parties and the dates, let them trace the lines of demarcation on a map. Let them struggle the way I had struggled with fascism—and let them worry about it!

The Oxbridge don, the one who had lectured during my first year at Yale, who had had his pencil poised in the question period for de Man's every word, now quoted from my book on fascist aesthetics in his article about the de Man scandal.

My happiness was complete.

Here is the irony. In my long article on de Man's wartime journalism, I didn't take sides. I said I didn't want to condemn or moralize, merely to describe. I set it out for all to see: the left-wing socialists who had turned to the right and made a national coalition in the interests of Belgian nationalism. The Flemish prejudice against the French. The contentment of the Belgians that the Germans had finally put one over on the French. At the end was my flourish of memory about de Man at Yale—remembering how he told us not to confuse theory with life. This is impossible advice, I said, implying that it was now difficult, if not impossible, to think about deconstruction without thinking about de Man's collaborationist past. That was where I ended—with impossibility and the confusion of theory and life.

Bill Golden wrote and said my historical research was useful, but he still wanted to know the answer to my flourish at the end: what part that job at the newspaper played in making de Man, the cool ironic theorist of language from whom we had tried to learn. "God, why did I always have the feeling he never talked to one," he wrote. That was Guy, not Bill—at the *very* moment when he's trying to say how angry he was that de Man had ignored him, he goes impersonal on his pronoun. Why, after all this time, couldn't he say, "the man never really talked to me"?

Dan wrote from his law practice in California to say that the news about de Man made his connection to literary criticism feel even more remote. He hadn't read de Man's wartime journalism yet, but from my description it sounded as though de Man had been misled by some backfiring idealism gone wrong. Wasn't I too easy on him, in my article? Didn't I have to pass judgment? Had I forgotten how suspicious everyone had been of my dissertation and wasn't I mad?

Someone at Yale called and said she admired the cool of my article but she could tell that I hadn't really loved him.

I had gone for the cool disinterest. At the moment of my greatest glee, the moment when I finally had something on my most enigmatic, famous teacher—just what I had always longed for!—I had reproduced the dry analysis, emotional deadpan, and the confusing flourish at the end. De Man's way.

"I've got it! I've got it!" I was screaming inside. But on the outside: "Well, you see, it goes like this . . . But please be patient, it's extremely complicated."

At Duke, the students were mad and excited and disgusted with us, their elders. "Jesus, theory is dead"—a woman named Serena. "It's corrupt, it's all based on shit!" They interviewed students and faculty to see what various people had to say about the scandal. There was the famous pragmatist on campus who said, well, World War II was the last time in American history that everyone agreed about who the good guys and bad guys were and, he concluded, this is what makes the scandal so satisfying—we are relieved to be thrust temporarily into the realm of good and evil again. A student started a correspondence with a reporter from *Time* who had written an article about the de Man scandal he disagreed with. Another student, cynical and wary, said that the de Man affair was an interpretive machine, that everyone would use it to do battle for their latest theory and that the whole event was a career opportunity for people desperate to publish.

Linda Orr—my first teacher at Yale and now my colleague—and I were teaching a seminar together on War and Memory, listening to all this talk, and I felt it coming back at me from them—my old struggle with teachers, wanting to know more about them than they knew about themselves.

For the first time, because of the de Man scandal, I was called on to narrate my own intellectual history. I needed to make the students understand, with only fifteen years' distance, what that atmosphere around deconstruction was, what I had learned from it, and how it made me react against them, with their consuming passion for history and politics and context. So much had changed.

Deconstruction was good for us. We were all reading the same books, trying to think together. It was an atmosphere of overwhelming curiosity and respect for the difficulty of thinking about literature. All that talk about "margins"—we knew we were at the *center* of intellectual life. We were sharpening our minds like razors, because we were the carriers of a new way of reading: the most advanced, thorough-going, questioning reading that had even been done on a text. Everything that has come since in literature—the smorgasbord of disciplines and methods that passes as "interdisciplinary work," the debate on the canon with its sad obsession with limited resources and turf—all seems unworthy by comparison. Deconstruction gave us a sensitivity to language, a need to look up close, and a sense that language is tricky—the ultimate adversary.

It was also bad for those reasons. The rigor about language constrained our imaginations. We suffered, because we thought there was only one way to be rigorous. That student who walked out of class—what was left for him, since he was outside the dominant conversation? And Guy, how many like him got too far into deconstruction, taking language apart into such tiny pieces that there was nothing left? If de Man had been a better teacher he would have seen the trouble Guy was having; he wouldn't have given up on pedagogy. De Man thought he had left persuasion behind for good in the War; he had fled a disaster of opinion, and opinion dogged him everywhere he went.

De Man would have been a better teacher if he had given more of his game away. He was Belgian. The problems he was interested in were related to Belgian culture, that odd mixture of Flemish and French elements and the conflicts of national identity that all got played out during the German Occupation. In his articles in *Le Soir*, de Man kept measuring the French national character against the German national character. We were getting the same debate in graduate school, the mixture of French and German texts I couldn't figure out. He didn't let on why he was attracted to those texts. Romanticism was the key to his thought—but why? Romanticism was at the root of fascism—giving one's self to the revolution, linking aesthetics and politics. He was working through his confusing relationship to European culture, being Flemish but French-educated. He was interested in autobiography—as an impossible genre, a kind of emblem of deconstruction, where the more you try to confess, the more you lie. The root of de Man's intellectual questions was in his own experience and pain.

Personal motivation. We didn't think about personal motivation. We thought of ourselves in the service of difficulty, absence, impossibility. The ground was too high; we couldn't possibly stay on it. We never thought about ourselves as writers. We were too literary. Curiosity about too many things was discouraged; author's lives, for example, were beneath us. We were told never to publish too soon, we were encouraged to take our time, endless time, because thinking was hard and exquisite. There weren't very many jobs, and of course we were there out of abstract dedication, not ambition. The standards made us miserable: we were a tense, ambitious, and fearful lot.

Guy didn't make it: he thought his dissertation had to be the shining truth and it ended up so difficult it was unreadable. He walked out of the classroom before he ever had to try his thinking in the world. His friends should have told him that what he was writing was unreadable. Not theoretically unreadable—plain unreadable.

"He didn't talk to one": Guy's memory of his attempts to talk to de Man, his thesis adviser, include two third-person and no first-person pronouns. Guy had the guts to walk out of his own class, years after the student with the Cross pen-and-pencil set walked out of our "Introduction to Literary Theory." My story isn't really that different from theirs, except that I waited longer to understand what the three of us had in common. De Man had failed me, too, only it was a failure that I wasn't aware of. I didn't go to talk to him, because I had no idea that he had given a minute's thought to the problem that interested me most—the problem of the fascist intellectual. He seemed the least interested of anyone on the faculty in that topic. Think of the questions I could have asked him, had I known to ask: Why did he think intellectuals had been attracted to fascism? Had he been attracted, or had he been doing hack work? What was it like to write for a newspaper controlled by the Nazis? What did he know about the camps? What role did personality play in people's attitude toward fascism? How did listening to the radio and going to the movies alter their perception of the world? What was it like living through the purge of the fifties? How did his guilt affect him?

I didn't talk to de Man, because none of my questions about fascism were on the horizon in New Haven in 1975—none were considered fit for literary theory as de Man defined it. What a waste! Taking apart meaning, looking at words, shunning the illusion of the fully present communicative voice—these aspects of deconstructionist theory as we absorbed it *may* have been part of de Man's intellectual struggle against the manipulative tendencies of fascist propaganda. *May* have: I'll never know, because de Man covered his work with the clean veil of disinterestedness. Now I'm helping my own Ph.D. students write their dissertations, and I don't want to fail them the way that de Man failed me. How do I tell them who I am, why I read the way I do?

What do students need to know about their teachers?

The Trouble with Edna

I have a student named Edna, who is doing an independent study with me on Jean-Marie Le Pen. She reminds me of myself when I was studying French poetry with Ann Smock, wanting her to see me as a serious person "working on literature."

Edna is just back from a year of study abroad where she took the majority of her classes at "Sciences Po"—the French institute for the study of political science. She is imbued with the style and the tone of a French Sciences Po student. She went even farther than I did to make herself over; her French is indistinguishable from that of a student at Sciences Po. She is every French professor's dream! She acquired all the micro-traits of intellectual francophilia: in her notebook, she underlines her main points, marked with Roman numerals "I.", "II.", "III.", in contrasting colored-pencil colors, and for every big point, she's got a little point "a.", a little point "b.", sub-points "i.", "ii.", "iii." This, I imagine, she got from sitting in French university amphitheaters where the professors actually say "aspect number three, second part, small a" as they're talking, to assist the students taking notes. Edna instructs me in our second work session that she wants to write her honors paper via the "Sciences Po" method. She's very attached to her pencils and to her pen, which she refers to as "mon bic."

Jean-Marie Le Pen, the object of her study, is a ruddy, wisecracking French politico and assemblyman, the leader and mastermind of an extreme right-wing party called the National Front. He's recycled some old slogans of the racist right, like "France for the French," and makes statements about wanting to kick all the Arab immigrants out of France and deport people with AIDS on trains. He provokes people to compare him to Hitler: AIDS in French is SIDA and Le Pen talks about AIDS patients as being "Sidaïque," which rhymes with "Judaïque"—Jewish. So the left press calls him a Nazi, and he tells them they're a bunch of over-interpreting intellectual losers with morbid one-track minds. The troubling part is that Le Pen has had a lot of support, both from disillusioned working-class communists and from high bourgeois types who are angry at the socialists, the immigrants, and the Jews. They like to watch Le Pen make a fuss.

The Edna with whom I speak about Le Pen in my office, in French, is entirely different from the whiny Edna who called me at home in English to ask in English to do the independent study in the first place. Her French is heavily intonated, clear as a bell, full of subjunctives. She addresses me as Madame. I suggest to her in our second meeting together that being an American may actually constitute an advantage for the study of Le Pen—that while she may prefer to write her essay in Sciences Po style, she should take advantage of her cultural remove from the material at hand, her American perspective. It was hard to even think of her as an American, the way she talked, but I said it anyway, to challenge her. She looked surprised, and I began to see, underneath the severe haircut, the military posture, the poised "bic," an eighteen-year-old kid grappling passionately with a newly formed intellectual identity.

I'm growing very fond of Edna—I'm starting to be able to tease her, she's starting to loosen up a bit, and we're starting to get some work done. She's going to do a "lexical study" of Le Pen, looking at the language in his speeches and how that language is received by the press, studying how the communist daily, L'Humanité, and the right-wing bourgeois daily, Le Figaro, and the socialist daily newspaper of record, Le Monde, quote him. In the guise of methodological assistance, I've had her reading Barthes' essays on cultural mythologies along with a book about Philippe Pétain's radio speeches and an article about Joan of Arc as a symbol of the right. She gobbles up this material and transposes her knowledge onto French graph paper (lines vertical and horizontal), main points double underlined, subordinate points single underlined with "le bic."

Edna is helping me think about the estrangement of working in French in American university French departments. What codes and tics and class prejudices we pass on to our students when we encourage them to speak "perfect French," whatever that is.

I read an interview in a big French daily paper with an American theater director working in Paris. This was a man who had lived in France for years and had worked his way through the system to the point of being made a director at the national theater, the Comédie Française. He directed, among other pieces of the patrimony, an ensemble of Molière farces. He stated in his interview that there was a moment in his life in France where he would rather have died than commit a grammar, a pronunciation, or an intonation mistake. During this period, he claimed, he had whipped his language into shapes and sounds that made it completely indistinguishable from native French. Finally "one day," as it were, he had some kind of cultural revelation and *reassumed* his accented French—the happy sign of his difference, which had always been his pleasure and his right.

American professors fought for a couple of generations to get out of the pigheadedness (pigheadedness picked up from the British) and laziness inherent in the idea that you could teach foreign literatures in English.

We would teach French language and French literature directly in French: everyone, from the first-semester student to the lecturer on Racine and Molière, was to function effortlessly in what language teaching specialists call, revealingly, the "target" language.

What is so bad about that? After all, isn't speaking French in the halls of an American university the *reward*, part of the aura and romance of going into French in the first place?

You can't work in a French department for long without wondering whether our attachment to French isn't pathological. Both the native speakers and the Americans suffer under a system where language skills are made a fetish. The "natives," who often arrive in this country as exiles under dramatic situations, have to come to terms with an isolation from their own culture, and learn to make a place for themselves in the American university, and in American intellectual life. What if their most passionate intellectual interests are untranslatable here? What if the debates in the English department next door make no room for them? The temptation is to cling to Paris, to take a colonizing attitude toward their role as purveyors of French culture. The system is complicated by issues of gender and sex roles. When I was a college student, I used to look around in my classes and wonder why the majority of the students in French—graduate and undergraduate—were female, yet most of the professors were male. Where were the missing bodies? Twenty years ago, it was commonplace for American men to marry French women they met on their year abroad. The women became their husbands' best editors and picked up extra money teaching language; the men became the literature professors. French departments divided up into "literature" sections—husbands—and less prestigious "language" sections—wives. While women now occupy more literature positions, the split between language and literature teaching, the disdain of the literati for the language instructors who make their own teaching possible—is still palpable in many French departments.

What about the ambiance of the French department? There are jokes in our field about male French professors who have worked in American French departments for ten years—brought here because of their scholarly prestige—and who still can't order a hamburger in English. They flourish in their workplace, the French department, where "French only" is a badge of honor. There is invariably trouble when a tyrannical or insensitive native speaker rules over a department where all the assistant professors are Americans, forever on guard against the telling mistake that might cost them a promotion. S, an American in her first job at an elite college, was asked by her native French chairman to take the minutes for the department meeting, held in French, and she worked on those minutes—which he called a *procès verbal* (the expression used for the transcript of a trial!)—for sixteen hours. One of the most important critics of modern French literature in the world likes to tell how he was denied tenure at another elite college because of his French "r," which smelled of New Jersey.

How can I explain to someone who doesn't function in this world the terror of the gender mistake: how I learned at the luncheon for my first campus visit job interview that pizza (why didn't I notice that characteristically feminine *a*-ending?) was feminine. Whether to call colleagues "vous" or "tu"? If you call them "vous" you are stuffy and formal; call them "tu" at the wrong moment you might be dressed down like an undergraduate. To be in French, you fold your stiff white shirt cuffs over your tight sweater cuffs; you cross your 7's, you can even say "hamburger" and "hot dog" and "Coca Cola" with a French accent.

French colleagues are invariably more generous in assessing the language skills of their American colleagues than we Americans are when we talk about each other ("Really, you know, her French isn't very good"). American French professors, they say, are much too self-conscious about petty details of linguistic performance, which have nothing to do with real intellectual life.

Easy for *them* to say: those details are our second identity.

When we started discussing the problem of what language to teach in at a French Civilization conference held in England, everyone got on edge, the whole tenor of the discussion changed: people started shouting, you felt the urgency and the desperation of their positions. I talked about Edna—my horror at feeling as though we American teachers of French only want to produce our own French fantasy, a kind of Stepford Wife, dressed as a Polytechnicienne. Is this horror just my stern Midwestern reaction? Do people in other fields have a stereotype to which they need to conform? (Or as Laurence Wylie put it at the conference, "Do you need an Oxford accent to study British history?") Is this a problem about how people learn, or is it about the furtive way that academics seek their social status? Other French professors attending the conference responded to these questions, sensibly, by invoking the "utility" argument: we don't have to make a fetish of French but we do have to teach people to function in the language; there is a basic level of functionality or utility toward which we can work. Adrian Rifkin, a British art historian and my kindred spirit in the group, responded passionately that there is no neutral "utility." Business French? The esthete's French, the kind they teach at the Ecole Normale? Technocrat's French (Polytechnique and Sciences Po)? Street French, the abject argot of a Céline? The zillions of ethnic Frenches—Canadian, Cajun ones, the French spoken in the northern suburbs of Paris by the beur, the North African immigrants. When a class of Duke students tells me that the Québécois have "bad accents" I know we've gone wrong with our utility argument. When they say that they want to speak "just like a real French person," I ask them: "Which one?"

This is a subject that touches American nerves because it touches our deep fear of not really speaking French that well, no matter how well we speak. While I was writing a book in French on Céline, the reference librarian in a major research library patiently explained to me, "here in France, our card catalogue lists books in alphabetical order." Do we end up picking up their disdain for us and making it ours?

There is that fear and humiliation, but also the pride at struggling against American ethnocentrism and enabling our students to speak and write in a language that's not their own.

Only a few students cross the barrier from wanting a good accent into real intellectual interests; they go to France and study political science and history and literature and then they come back to us. Like Edna.

Edna is my conscience, my whole *métier* speaks to me through the person of Edna.

Edna came into my office yesterday. It was raining cats and dogs outside. Edna said, "Bonjour Madame. Il fait un temps bien Belge" (what Belgian weather we're having). The idiom is a Belgian joke, the French equivalent of the Polish joke. It's relatively insignificant on the scale of ethnic slurs—after all, it does rain more in Belgium than in France—but hearing Edna say it made me wince. She had come to study Le Pen and his slurs, not to make slurs of her own.

Edna, discarding, borrowing, and passing in French, reminds me of the time I said "Que je suis bête!" to a French novelist and feminist philosopher, Monique Wittig. I knew her essay on "The Mark of Gender," about pronouns and the normative use of the third person singular "he." Wittig argues that when you use "he" in sentences in the place of "she" (for example: "the American citizen must know that *his* rights are inalienable"), you're not merely trying to make life easier by eliminating a superfluous pronoun, you're accepting that the male pronoun, the "he"—and hence, by implication, the male—is the universal subject. "He" represents both "he" and "she": "she" is an afterthought. The theory is her linguistic activism.

Wittig and I had both showed up for a lecture in the wrong room. We were looking through the door at the empty amphitheater. "Que je suis bête," how stupid I am to have forgotten the room number, I said, lapsing—with a rising intonation that Micheline once taught me to practice

—into my ordinary-French-person, pass-the-time-away speech. Wittig looked at me in shock, she took in each word seriously and saw that the words and the deed didn't correspond. "No, you're not stupid," she said, concerned. I had put on my Bordeaux matron sociolect, and it came out sounding like a dubbed version of TV's "Dallas," high and slightly affected: "OOOOH, how steouupid of me!" Monique Wittig, for whom verbal style signifies, was not going to let my cliché pass unnoticed. She looked at me in a way that said, "kill the language that makes us dumb." The cliché was the price I was willing to pay for that perfect bit of intonation. Like Edna today. Wittig wasn't buying it—nor should I.

While I am thinking all this, Edna is laughing at her own opening remark in such an embarrassed way that I suspect the absurdity of a North Carolina Belgian joke has struck her, too; perhaps she'd reached a crossroad during the work of the previous week. Sure enough, for the first time, she pulls out an article from the New York Times, an article by Richard Bernstein on Le Pen which she had underlined in sea green. She's "broken a rule" by letting herself read in English. "Finally," she tells me, "I've found an article that actually deals with the speech of Le Pen. Those articles from the daily French press are so useless, so clichéd—'Where is Le Pen now?' 'Where is he going?' 'Where will he be in five years?'—whereas Bernstein has had time to think about it. He analyses Le Pen's way of speaking . . . he understands that Le Pen manipulates through a language style." Edna hands me the Bernstein article, I read it, and as the talk goes on, I realize we have slipped quite happily into English.

" 'Sidaïque,' 'Judaïque': Why are the form and the sound of a word so powerful?"

" 'Sidaïque' has the memory of 'Judaïque' in it—the memory of the deportations."

"He dishes it out with that smile."

It was our first intellectual conversation in English. I remember some of the English words she used; the phrase "my French granny" in particular, which came up in the context of an old lady in Paris who had lent Edna books to read. Does she have an actual French grandmother, or did she adopt an alternative French family, like so many of us francophiles do? The word *granny* sounded so American: I wondered what made her think about her granny in her own tongue. Speaking to Edna in English for the first time was charged, charmed, as though our native English had gained from our relationship to French all the clarity and peculiarity of a mastered foreignness.

It didn't matter what language we were speaking, Edna and I, for the rest of the semester, because there were ideas and problems we were passionate about that we were trying to learn about together. We'd switch languages in midstream; we'd quote English phrases in French and French phrases in English; on Tuesday we'd speak in English, on Wednesday entirely in French.

In the end we weren't speaking in one language or the other—we were speaking to each other:

"I know why I like making Belgian jokes—they make me feel so . . . French!"

The Interview

As an American student in France in the years 1973–74, I had been closed off from the French students who might, in another context, have been my friends. French students with my political affinities were profoundly anti-American because of their opposition to our war in Vietnam. I saw more of their graffiti than of them. It took a certain kind of political conservatism, or accidents of family and class, to open up a twenty-year-old French person to friendships with Americans. People my age who spent a year in France report the same experience: it was North Africans who were friendliest, most open. Oddly enough we had a lot in common, the students who had come to France after decolonization and the Americans who had come to France to get themselves some culture.

The minute I became a professor everything changed for me in my relationship to France. Those students who had remained strangers to me, hidden in their Grandes Ecoles and Facultés, studying for their exams, writing their theses, were now my colleagues, friendly and curious about the research going on in American universities.

I discovered this fact rather startlingly a year after completing my dissertation and taking my first job. My new colleagues introduced me to a complex Parisian network of friends of colleagues, apartment exchanges, and name after name of people to look up on future trips to France. This network, the security of a salary, and the means to travel made me start to think about France as a living library, an enormous proving ground for my thesis.

I would start by making contact with people who had played a role in the 1930s. But the fascist intellectuals I had written about were dead. Drieu la Rochelle, the most decadent of the lot, had committed suicide at the end of the war; Brasillach, an esthete literary critic who had edited the most vicious of the fascist weekly newspapers, was executed for treason in 1945; Céline had died of an aneurysm in 1961. On my first research trip to France as a professional scholar in the summer of 1982, I set out to find the only fascist intellectual discussed in my dissertation who was still alive; his name was Maurice Bardèche. Bardèche was the keeper of the archives of the executed writer Robert Brasillach; he had been Brasillach's best friend at the Ecole Normale and had married Brasillach's sister, Suzanne. At the end of the war Bardèche, like Brasillach, was arrested and imprisoned. He had been a tenured professor at the University of Lille; he was stripped of his title. After his brother-in-law Brasillach was executed, Bardèche went off the deep end. He wrote pamphlets against the Liberation, against the purge of fascists, against the Nuremberg war crime trials. He denounced the Jews; he doubted the truth of the Holocaust. In the first book he published after the war, Nuremberg ou la terre promise, he maintained that the gas chambers were museum pieces set up by the Allies to destroy the German spirit. He helped found the genre now known widely as Revisionism or, more accurately, Negationism.

Negationism comes in different flavors: fascist, anti-Zionist, American, French. In 1980, the French intellectual world was shaken when a literature professor named Robert Faurisson started publishing revisionist articles. Partly in response to the Faurisson scandal, the French historian Vidal-Naquet wrote an essay called "A Paper Eichmann" in which he presented a checklist of the basic tenets that were cropping up in the burgeoning negationist output, including Faurisson's:

1. There was no genocide of Jews, Gypsies, etc., in World War II; the instrument symbolizing genocide—the gas chamber—never existed.

2. The "final solution" was only intended as a relocation of Jews to their "home" territory in Eastern Europe.

3. The number of victims of the camps is more like fifty thousand than the six million that are claimed. The deaths were natural, due to allied bombings or to "facts of war."

4. Nazi Germany either is not responsible for the outbreak of World War II, or it shares that responsibility equally with the Jews.

5. The major enemy of humankind in the 1930s and 1940s wasn't Hitler's Germany but Stalin's USSR.

6. Genocide is an invention of allied propaganda, inspired by Jews and the Zionist agenda; the figure six million is linked to the Jewish propensity for false statistics such as those found in the Talmud.

I wrote to Maurice Bardèche in the spring of 1982 with a queasy stomach, knowing whom I was writing to, but ambitious to see him. The heart of darkness wrote back by return mail; of course I was welcome. He would be at the family vacation house in Canet Plage, near Perpignan. I could take a hotel room on the beach.

I stared at Bardèche's friendly letter, full of the warm formulae that French writers trade in with such ease. "Chère Alice Kaplan," it read, in his hand, and as I read I said to myself that my last name was the same as that of the Grand Rabbin, the head rabbi of France. An unmistakably Jewish name. A Jew being welcomed by a fascist. Maybe the labels didn't mean anything anymore? I was going to find out if they did.

On my way to Canet I stopped in Orléans to see a friend of my teacher Linda Orr's, Claude Mouchard, a poet and critic who shared her interest in history and revolution, who, Linda told me, would share my interest in the 1930s. We sat in a walled garden in the back of his rambling house.

Our talk soon turned soon to my intellectual reasons for being in France: the visit to Bardèche. Claude reacted to my announcement coolly, telling me about Bardèche's edition of Balzac. He laughed about the fact that Bardèche had a fairly decent reputation as a literary critic in spite of his politics.

Then he shifted in his seat: "You know of course that his brother-in-law, Brasillach, and his newspaper were responsible for the assassination of Hélène's father."

Hélène, Claude's wife, was in the kitchen.

He filled in the history. Hélène Mouchard was born Hélène Zay; her father was Jean Zay, Minister of Education in the 1930s, who was imprisoned by the Vichy government during the Occupation. He was finally taken out of prison under false pretenses in 1944 and murdered by a group of men disguised as Resistance fighters who were part of a thug squad called the "Milice"—a fascist law-and-order gang who scrounged around doing evil in the last years of the war. The newspaper *Je Suis Partout*, edited by Robert Brasillach, had called for the death of the Popular Front ministers, and these thugs had taken them up on it. Now as I sat in the garden I remembered Jean Zay's name from right-wing Vichy propaganda that I had pored over, and from Céline, who had made the name into a famous pun: Je vous Zay (for "Je vous hais"—I hate you).

"Have you thought about what it means to even agree to talk with this man? There has to be an ethics for your interview—you have to formulate an ethics for the situation you're going into. Have you considered it fully?"

A hundred thoughts went through my mind in response to Claude's challenge. Ethics? Does ethics mean my behavior? Does it mean I have to decide how I'm going to react to Bardèche before I've even met him? Am I not allowed to smile? Should I shake his hand? None of these thoughts had occurred to me before, in any detail; I had been too determined to get the interview in the first place. Maybe that was for the better, I thought. Shouldn't I be open to surprises? Isn't the point that I don't have to have a prepared response, that I should be ready for the accidents of a real conversation? On the other hand, maybe Claude Mouchard was offering me something with this idea of ethics. A French person couldn't go to see Bardèche the way I was going; the visit itself would be a declaration of affinity. It was as though, in France, the events of the war had happened very recently; nor was this the first time I had noticed how raw the subject remained in daily life. Why did my national removal make my situation any different? Was I going to see the equivalent of a Lieutenant Calley, or a Richard Nixon, or some old crank revisionist—a French Arthur Butz—who happened to have gone to Harvard?

I don't know what I would have said to Claude at that moment if Hélène Mouchard, born Hélène Zay, hadn't come into the garden, leaving his question hanging in midair. In a sense I wasn't ready to answer his question; I was too young and too eager for my interview and too hungry to learn everything I could about France, by observing. The thought of an ethics stayed in my head that summer, and returns periodically to haunt me. What does it mean for a Jewish intellectual to work on fascism? Is my role that of a prosecutor or that of a spy? What produces my energy for this kind of work? What is in it for me?

Claude Mouchard was my guide on a long afternoon walk through Orléans, the city that Joan of Arc had liberated from the English in 1429. Our conversation twisted and turned, in a way that was very foreign to me then and since has become one of rituals of French intellectual life I enjoy most. Mouchard and I continued to circle back to Bardèche as we commented on the space around us. What are the ethics of interviewing Bardèche? How can you do it? See here this statue of Joan of Arc, it represents a right-wing France, the France of Bardèche; do you recognize the images of Marianne, symbol of the Republic, she represents the left, she is the symbol of Hélène's family. I will never forget the difference between Joan of Arc and Marianne as I learned it that afternoon. One a boyish, straight-haired innocent warrior, the other lush and wavy-haired and passionate. I was hungry to see the places, the traces of the ideologies referred to in the hundreds of pages of literary criticism and history I had read at Yale. Claude was a compelling if didactic guide. I surprised him by what I didn't know. *Il m'a fait la leçon.*

In Canet, the morning of my first interview, I was too restless to stay at my hotel, so I walked around the old part of town until it was time for my lunch date at the Bardèche cottage. Walking through the market, I saw coming toward me an old man with a big crater in the middle of this forehead and a shopping basket in his hand. I thought, that guy looks like a war criminal if there ever was one—a week in France without speaking a word of English, anticipating the meeting, had put me in a melodramatic frame of mind. When I showed up at the bungalow it was Bardèche; he was the man with a crater in the middle of his forehead.

"Oh, it's you," I said, surprised, and he didn't understand how I seemed to recognize him, even though we had never met.

"A first scene in a movie," I thought.

The hole in the head came up again in conversation; Bardèche referred to it fondly, pointing to himself. He had gotten it as the result of an auto accident in the 1950s; his family teased him, in front of me, that it had worked like a lobotomy, because it had calmed him down from his anger of the postwar purge years, when he was denouncing everyone and everything.

What no one in the family was saying was that he was still angry, but he had found other, more devious channels for unleashing his anger on the world. He was extremely subtle. He behaved like a very generous, very distinguished professor, with marvelous stories he was willing to share. I spent three days at that bungalow, interviewing Bardèche in his study. I asked him about his attraction to 1930s fascism, his views about cinema (he had co-authored an important early film history with his ill-fated brother-in-law), the purge of collaborators after the war, his career as a belated fascist polemicist. He hadn't been allowed to teach in forty years, he was dying to teach, he missed the amphitheater at Lille, full of students during the war. There were moments of remarkable human sympathy. Weren't we simply two people working together, listening to each other? When he said, laughing, about a specific sentence in one of his books, "that's precisely the genre of absolute sentence I'm in the habit of writing," I laughed back. I wasn't thinking about ethics—I was enjoying his self-mockery.

I ate lunch each day with the extended family. There were children my age, who teased me about why in the world I wanted to talk to their crazy father; there were grand-children and au pairs and family friends, all gathered on a vine-covered veranda. Sardines cooking over a grill on grapevine wood. On the third day of the interviews, I arrived at the cottage with a contribution to lunch: a plum tart, the biggest I could find at the market.

Bardèche's wife Suzanne said, "Robert loved these plums." There was a respectful silence at the table. I understood that she lived with her dead brother every day, he was there at the table.

I had no ethics to guide me. I was listening; maybe I was neutral. I was as young as I would ever be as a French professor. My father was there with me—in my head, I mean. He was light brown, brown in his suit with his sandy hair. He was giving me advice: "Take it slow, just let him talk . . . Now, now's the time to step in, give him an opening."

My father was running his hand through his hair the way I do, feeling for his thoughts: "If you let him keep talking you'll learn something new." He was my age, the young prosecutor at Nuremberg wearing his headphones, the man with the intense gaze whom I knew from a framed news-paper clipping, taken from a Czech newsmagazine. He had earphones on to hear the testimony. He was listening, he was intensely focused, but I couldn't tell what he thought.

So on we went, Bardèche and I, in our game. I didn't talk about being Jewish—I didn't want to give him an opening. Nor did I fight with him, about fascism or anything else. I knew his line: I didn't want to raise our passions, when there was no hope of my changing his views nor any danger that his views could win out. He was a museum piece; I was the curator. He, in turn, was delicate with me, dancing only on the edge of his Holocaust revisionism by referring obliquely to Free Speech—and how Americans know well enough to protect it.

He was working as hard as he could to get me to like him. He told me a long pathetic story about his attraction to the Jewish quarter in Paris, wandering outside the temple after sabbath services in the fifties—when he was reviled throughout all of France as an anti-Semite—but what he was doing was admiring the Jewish girls with their freckles—not pretty, necessarily, but so appealing! He wasn't going to let me get any closer to his anti-Semitism than this bit of philo-Semitism, but it was close enough. My tape recorder whirred away in the background, and I rubbed my freckled nose in nervous excitement. As the afternoon sun shone in the windows on his walls of books and papers, I saw myself in his study as a professor doing important historical fieldwork; through the passing of time together and the growing familiarity of our conversation, Bardèche had ceased to be the person whose most deeply felt ideas horrified me.

When I think about that summer in France, my first summer as a professor, I see the Mouchard and the Bardèche families sitting on benches, facing each other, introducing me to intellectual life in the country I had chosen to study. I see the righteousness of the Mouchards and the seductive charm of the Bardèches. I see the body of Robert Brasillach, Bardèche's brother-in-law, hanging from the execution post in 1945, and I see the body of Jean Zay, Hélène's father, rotting in a ditch. I see my father, sitting at the Nuremberg trials with his earphones on, listening, but telling me nothing.

When I got back from France in September I transcribed my most interesting conversations with Bardèche. I sat at my desk with headphones on and listened to my voice— the innocent sound of it in French, and the "hmmm"s I produced, like an analyst, when I didn't like what Bardèche was saying but didn't want to cut him off. I talked through my introduction to the interview with Linda Orr, line by line, thought by thought. She challenged me, differently than her friend Claude had done, by urging me to put into writing the contradictions and challenges of the situation—not to make it too "clean," or resolved. It was Linda Orr who helped me understand, when I was most agonized about what to say, that writing isn't a straight line but a process where you have to get in trouble to get anywhere. Because I was disturbed, it was better writing than any I had done before.

My interview with Maurice Bardèche appeared as an article and as the last chapter of a book, both with Bardèche's permission. He was an impeccable collaborator, had for years published his own journal—a raving extremist journal, but a journal nonetheless, and was extremely comfortable with the rituals of proofreading, giving permissions. His correspondence with my editors was punctual and clear.

In November 1985, as my book on fascism was going to press, my working relationship with Bardèche having come to a tidy end, I received a four-page handwritten letter from him with this cover note attached:

> Dear Alice Kaplan, I hesitate to send you the letter that is attached to this note. I am afraid that it might cause you pain. Remember, even if it irritates you, that I have much sympathy for you and much confidence in you. That is why I've written it. You must not be afraid of the truth of others; you must try to understand.

Is it too banal, too obvious, to point out that going to interview Bardèche had put me in a daughterly role? I had sought out the relationship; he had welcomed it. Now he was going to get me back for what he had given.

The anger and disgust he had hidden so successfully was right there for me to see in the four pages that followed his note, beginning with his frustration about all that we hadn't said at Canet Plage. He was setting out to haunt me, and to block me from thinking back on him with any peace of mind:

> You see, dear Alice Kaplan, how right you are in your reflections on the interviews. It's worse than you think. Because, after the interviews, there are letters. Not only is the monster not as monstrous as you thought, but he speaks. Not only does he speak, but he takes his tools out of his toolbox like an electrician who is going to do repairs. It's hideous.

He referred to me as an "anthropologist of anti-Semitism" and to himself as the "Negro." Like all American professors, he claimed, I believed that the Frenchmen who lived through the Occupation were "Negroes," who thought and felt like "Negroes," with brains and sensibilities absolutely foreign to those of a good American. He was going to give me some indications about the "Negro"—about him—that might be useful to me:

1. No French intellectual knew about the existence of the concentration camps, he began.

2. Jews died, because of allied bombings, because of disease; that was not the fault of the Nazis.

3. Painful as it is to acknowledge, there can be, and was, extermination *without will to exterminate*. "Pas de volonté d'extermination": no will to exterminate.

Bardèche was offering me, a Jew, the Holocaust without guilt. "The Jews just died like flies," he said; "how I hesitate to cause you pain." He insisted on the "martyrdom" of all his negationist comrades, like Robert Faurisson, who were being punished for announcing the truth, as he had been when he published *Nuremberg ou la terre promise*. He punctuated his letter with the ghoulish form of address, "chère Alice Kaplan," as though repeating my name over and over made his sentences carry further, because they were addressed to a Jew.

The horrible gist of it, as far as I was concerned, was not that he had written a negationist polemic—he had written many of those, the details of this one came as no surprise to me—but that he would address his revisionism directly to me, fashioning it, personalizing it, as a result of the complicity we had established in our interview.

In the ending flourish to his letter, he let me know he understood a thing or two about me, about my desire to be accepted in France and my need for camouflage:

196

"If once again, you get the chance to be French for a little while, come see us."

When Bardèche's letter came I traveled quickly back to that day when I was eight, so powerful in my imagination that I often think it the basis of my entire sense of history, when I violated the privacy of my dead father's desk drawers and found the evidence from Nuremberg: photos from Auschwitz. Evoking those pictures with my eight-year-old self-consciousness, the horror came back, the horror of being too young to live with this much horror, too young to have a dead father. Then, returning to my adulthood I measured my father's absence again, its twenty-year duration. My father hadn't been there to kill the bats; he hadn't been there to explain the photographs of Auschwitz; he wasn't there to tell me what to say to Bardèche. I understood how much I owed to his death, his absence a force field within which I had become an intellectual; his image, silent and distant with headphones over his ears, a founding image for my own work. Headphones were also an emblem for loneliness and isolation: they transmitted voices, they absorbed testimony; but they had no voice to give back.

I still have a photocopy of my response to Maurice Bardèche's letter, as superficial as I could make it—I wasn't going to pour my heart out to someone who had just knifed me—and as beside the point, with only an allusion or two to what I really thought in case he cared to read between the lines. "As you must imagine," I wrote,

> I was very struck by your letter, not only by your enormous talent as a propagandist—in spite of the fact and also *because* it is Alice Kaplan that you're going after—but

also by everything you say about the 'bad anthropology' of my text. Seeing yourself in black and white, desiccated and reconstructed in the service of a theory of literary fascism, must be annoying and even disagreeable. Please accept, dear Maurice Bardèche, the expression of my cordial salutations and my thanks, once again, for all that you have taught me.

Alice Kaplan

I put my response in the mail; it was the last communication I had with Bardèche. I put Bardèche's four-page letter to me in a file marked "Bardèche." I put the file in a storage box. I piled the storage box with several others in a crevice behind a brick chimney in my bedroom. It took me five years to decide to reread the letter and forty-five minutes to dislodge the storage box from its crevice. I had forgotten most of the details: the comparison Bardèche makes between himself and "Negroes" (accusing me of exploiting him); the references to Jews dying like flies (implying sub-mammalian genetic weakness); the phony wish not to hurt me as he is attacking me, the knowing cut in the end about my wanting to be French. I asked Philippe Roussin, a friend and colleague with whom I was working on Céline, to read the letter out loud during one of our dinners so that I could listen to its intonations through his native inflection. He was a good actor: he read the letter like an aged pedagogue, caressingly paternalistic, with a growling, sadistic undertone to his voice (my image of the professor in Ionesco's *The Lesson*). I put my hand over my mouth, stifled shrieks, laughed in disgust, and shuddered. After he had finished, I grabbed the letter out of his hand and pushed it aside, dangerously close to a glass of icewater. There was nothing more to say.

"Don't get it wet," he said, "you may want to give it to the Center for Jewish Documentation in Paris . . . it's a classic racist document."

I've rewritten the story of my first research trip to France several times, with slightly different emphases and different "morals"—from empathy to vengeance—based on the same structure. Mouchard and Bardèche are polar opposites, Marianne and Joan of Arc. Mouchard/Marianne is rigid, didactic, judgmental, or else a beacon of intellectual virtues, who doesn't hesitate to challenge the views of a young colleague whose project he takes seriously—and personally. Bardèche/Joan of Arc is, in turn, sadistic, psychotic, manipulative, tragic. Linda Orr and Claude Mouchard are another polarized duo, representing the freedom of writing versus the constraints of ethics, but also two different intellectual styles: in shorthand, American and French. I am naive, calm, omniscient, duped, manipulative, powerless, or cannily silent, depending. My father is always in the wings.

Bardèche's last letter to me almost succeeded in its goal: I hid it because I dreaded rereading it, or writing about it. Since retrieving it, however, I've rewritten the chapter again, making him more evil, more monstrous, conforming to the portrait he paints of himself: "The monster speaks! It's hideous." His avuncular charm has faded.

The opposing players in my drama, the Mouchards and the Bardèches, have only one trait in common: they both survived losses brought on by the Second World War. 1945, 1945: why does it feel so close, why am I still fighting the battles of another time and place, as though they were mine? What do I have in common with those families? In a dream sequence in my imaginary movie about my trip to Canet, I run back to Bardèche's study and challenge him; tell him I despise him, that he is lying, that he can't face the truth of his own guilt. I refuse to eat with his family, out of ethics. I put on my headphones, and I put him on the stand.

Returning Home

I'm not writing only about French anymore. French is the mark of something that happened to me, that made me shift into another language. Was it my father? Why do I keep circling in my work around intellectual men and their political crimes, their innocent or noble or charming surfaces and their shameful undersides?

One day I remembered that my father's nickname for me was Alkie. I had been working on my memoir for several years, so I was in the business of such details. Why hadn't I made a place in my story for his name for me? Alkie, a Jewish name. Also Alkie, short for alcoholic.

I called my mother.

"Why did he call me Alkie and why did he drink?"

"Guess he did call you that occasionally. It's a Jewish name or something. You know you were always such an engaging child, we adored you."

"So how did his drinking affect his personality?"

"It didn't really; it didn't have any effect on his work."

"Didn't the smell bother you?"

"I was used to the smell of tobacco and alcohol."

"Didn't it affect your sex life?"

"Oh, you develop a tolerance. It's people who don't drink who can't tolerate it, you know; people who drink can drink an enormous amount and it doesn't bother them."

"So if it had no effect, what were you so worried about all the time?"

"Because it was killing him. You don't understand, he wasn't the kind of person you could tell what to do. If a person doesn't want to stop you can't make them. It's like Nancy Everett who came to dinner the other night. She's huge. She knows it. But she's not ready to do something about it. You can't make someone . . . Look, what you have to understand were the times. Everyone drank, since Prohibition ended, it was a novelty. Of course, no one knew then how bad it was for the heart. We made all those drinks, Pink Ladies. I could make all those drinks. And I hated the cocktail parties—there was never anything to eat, I used to get so hungry. Once in Washington they served Martinis and I got such bad indigestion I had to take a taxi home. It was the times—everyone in Washington drank."

"I'm not interested in the times, I'm interested in our family. People aren't alcoholics because of the times."

"Yes they are, Alice, yes they are."

I started talking to everyone in my family. I talked to people on the phone, I called them up and took notes, as though it were an interview. I filled legal pads. My sister was appalled when I told her I had written down what she said.

"You're turning the family into a research project—I don't want to be an object for your study. And you didn't even tell me you were doing it until after. It's underhanded. And it's cold."

But I didn't feel cold, I was burning.

One day I went to the library meaning to prepare a course

and stayed there all day, looking up stray details from my father's work life in the *New York Times Index*, the newspaper microfilm, in indexes from books about Joseph McCarthy. Before I was born, he had defended a man named "Scientist X," charged with spying—I looked up the accounts. The only book which mentioned my father was the account of an incident from the 1930s, a Rutgers professor was fired by his Nazi department head and my father had defended him, *pro bono*, for the ACLU. My father was not a hero in the book. His statements were a little too grandiose, and he settled too soon. The authors concluded that he must have had a lot of other work to do.

Everyone in the family remembers my father working at the dining room table after dinner, his legal pads spread out all over the table. Even though he had his own study, he liked to be there, right in the middle of us, working, showing who he was, how impressive, Harvard Law Review, lost in his own world right in our midst.

We share a Phi Beta Kappa pin, "Sidney Joseph Kaplan, University of Minnesota, 1928" engraved on one side and "Alice Kaplan, University of California, 1975" engraved on the other. The man who could go to a symphony and come home and play the music on the piano by ear. The man who could win an argument in law school class against Felix Frankfurter—someone even wrote about it in a remembrance of Frankfurter and my brother sent me the article when I became a professor; at the time I cried in a mix of competitive longing and grief and I thought, "This is who my father was, a man who could take on Supreme Court justices when he was twenty."

Learning French was connected to my father, because French made me absent the way he was absent, and it made me an expert the way he was an expert. French was also a response to my adolescence, a discipline to cover up the changes in my body I wanted to hide. My mother had a lot to say about that:

"So why didn't you tell me when you got your period—god, you were strange."

"Well, you were strange, too, Mom, you were strange, too."

During these long conversations my mother and I kept calling each other "strange" in order to say that we thought the other person hadn't understood:

"Look, I'm the one with the tragic childhood, not you. My mother had a nervous breakdown when I was three, and she went away to a hospital for two years. An older cousin came from New York to take care of us. None of my sisters even remember, but I used to lie in bed at night and worry that my mother was going to die."

"That's funny, I used to worry you'd die, too."

"Then when mother came home she was so vain, she stood in front of the mirror for hours and tried all her clothes on."

"I know, you told me that."

"Oh, and you know I used to hate those office cocktail parties. I used to call up to see if he had been drinking and if he had I was panicked about him driving home and I used to drive downtown to the office—I drove in those days—and picked him up. I was afraid if he drove home he'd kill somebody. My friend Loretta was saying the other day how great those cocktail parties were. I didn't say anything. They were horrible."

"So tell her, mom."

"I think I'll call her up and tell her."

*   *   *

One weekend I flew home to talk to my father's brother for the first time in fifteen years. I had never talked to him about my father. I stayed with my cousin Ann, who dug up old photographs, including a letter my father had written to this brother at the height of the Depression, advising him not to go live in Paris:

> With all its excellence, Europe has absolutely nothing to add in the way of background to a man who is not in a position to spend a great deal for it and pay for it. Poverty in Europe would defeat the primary purposes of your plan. I know, although as you know, I have never been there.

and

> What would it avail to eat and sleep in Paris (if that) if you could not avail yourself of what Paris has to offer? What good to be in France if you were tied down to a 4 × 8 room with a bug-ridden bed in a "pension"— if you couldn't travel—if you couldn't attend L'Opera or L'Opera Comique when you reasonably wanted to—if you didn't have the price of the requisite number of "aperitifs" at the Cafe de la Paix or any other cafe you felt like sitting at. What good the whole damned works if you didn't have the margin d'argent to afford you that minimum flexibility to make the whole experience a liberalizing influence.

His little brother took his advice and stayed home. My father, who was six years older and already working, eventually supported him through law school. I wonder if my father would have wanted me to go to Europe? What would life have been like? Would we have been very rich (like Mr. D)? What would it have been like to rebel against a real father (like my sister got to do), instead of inventing an imaginary one? And would I have had the same suspicions, the same secrets, would I have even wanted to know French?

When my brother read my father's letter he was struck like me by all the envious detail about Paris, the Café de la Paix and the Opéra and the size of the room, and as a kind of afterthought, he said to me: "Remember, they used to speak to each other in French all the time when they didn't want us to understand."

"What do you mean? They didn't know any French."

"Oh, yes they did, they used their college French, they used to say things all the time right in front of us."

If I try really hard, I can just remember what their college French sounded like, their funny flat "r"s and the high-minded tone. And then it fades away.

While I was home that weekend I went out to the lake where I grew up and I talked to the people who live in the lake house now. I took a photograph of the water in the exact spot where the dock had been, where my father and I were together in the minutes before he died. In the photo I took, the lake looks dark and churning and a little oily, from all the motorboats. I remembered my father now, not just the monument I built to house him. I remembered his slow deliberateness; I remember not knowing whether he was slowing down for me, a child, or whether he was trying to cover up the clumsiness of a few too many drinks. I remember his voice, too, every syllable stretched out and the raspiness of tobacco in it. I see myself back there on the dock the day of my eighth birthday, the day of his funeral, trying to paint the trees across the water, and mad, because I couldn't get my trees to look like the real ones.

Afterwards

The first day of class. I look out over my classroom. Most of the students are just back from their junior year. They have that look—the way they wear their clothes and part their hair. I see it in their eyes, they're transformed, they want me to help them keep it all going.

I haven't been in France for six months and I'm rusty, I'm out of shape for French. I'm in the middle of a sentence and I wonder how I'm going to get to the end, my intonation is off a little and I hear some air in my "p"s. I start correcting myself, I'm feeling double. I say the ritual words, a welcome to the course, and I settle down. I'm in my French persona.

In graduate school one of our classmates took an overdose of insulin and went into a coma; when he came out, he had severe brain damage. His name was Larry. He couldn't speak much at all and when we visited him we tried speaking to him in French. We wanted to think that the French was hidden safe somewhere inside him, waiting for us to coax it out. But he had lost his French completely.

Why did I think of him just now, when I'm so near the end of my story? Because sometimes I don't want to need French so much. I want to be free of it. No more secret language, no more veering off, no more wanting in and never quite getting there. Because I can't imagine not having French. I think I would starve without it.

I can't stand not to be in France in June, the month of my birthday and the month my father died. The smells and sounds in the air are too strong at home—the newly cut grass, the fireflies, all the sounds of his death. So every year around the same time, I start speaking to myself in French and dreaming in French, and swearing in French when I'm driving my car. Maybe this book will put a stop to it.

When I took a group of students to Paris for the first time in June of 1988, I wanted to control their experience. Obligatory walks. A scavenger hunt. Look what I saw! Love what I loved! I wanted them to have experiences in French. They looked back at me with their amused eyes and they gave me a name, MadKap, short for Madame Kaplan. MadKap in French is "tourbillon," a spinning top. It was good to be alive with them and answer to the name they gave me.

In France I gave the women a big speech about flat shoes, quoting Simone de Beauvoir in The Second Sex on how even the right to walk through the city was denied to women. The women in our Duke-in-Paris program have problems making their way through the city. They are constantly harassed. Their language method books don't prepare them for the kind of dialogue they need. Sherri and Jerry come up with the right method: You look up really mean at the person who's harassing you, you look him right in the face, and you say in the snootiest sixteenth-arrondissement accent you can muster, "On se connaît?" (Do we know one another?)

Every week the students turn in their diary pages, reporting on their adventures in the city, their sentences, and through them I relive my own discovery of France.

208

It is exciting to be there, *là-bas*, the object of our study is all around us and not an ocean away. The books I assign are in the bookstore down the street, they don't need to be ordered six months in advance; the museums have the art evoked in the books and the books have places in them you can go to, a metro stop away. Paris is the uncontested capital of French intellectual life and its districts and history are all laid out for us to see; we can even read about the cafés we're sitting in as we sit in them. At last I am working in the place I am working on. At home, I think, I am envious of my friends in the English department who teach their own national literature. They are connected, they are in the fray, and I am removed. Here I feel at peace, not split in two.

Why do people want to adopt another culture? Because there's something in their own they don't like, that doesn't *name them.*

French still calls out to me in the most primitive way. If I'm in a crowded room and there are two people speaking French all the way on the other side of the room, I'll hear, loud as day, as though a friend were calling my name. My ears prick up. I become all ears, hearing every word, noticing the words I don't know or haven't heard for a while and remembering when I last heard them. I'll eavesdrop shamelessly, my attention now completely on that conversation, as if I belong in it; I'll start trying to figure out how to get in on it.

I go back and forth in my thinking about my second language. Sometimes I think, it's only the wealthy students who get French; it's only an expression of their class privilege. My privilege that I went away to Europe when I was fifteen and the shape of my mouth and the sounds going in and out

209

of my ears weren't frozen into place yet. An accident of class. Or, I think, why have I confined myself to teach in this second language, this language which will never be as easy as the first one? Why have I chosen to live in not-quite-my-own-language, in exile from myself, for so many years—why have I gone through school with a gag on, do I like not really being able to express myself?

Then something will happen, in the classroom, and I'll see this French language as essential in its imperfection: the fact that we don't have as many words is forcing us to say more. The simplicity of our communication moves us, we're outside of cliché, free of easy eloquence, some deeper ideas and feelings make it through the mistakes and shine all the more through them.

In French class I feel close, open, willing to risk a language that isn't the language of everyday life. A sacred language.

It is hard to separate what happens in French class from what happens in reading literature in French, in an intellectual tradition that is so sensitive to the nuances of language. It has to do with that shift in identification that goes along with studying literature, where you're able to feel close to a character who isn't you. A conservative fraternity student broke into English the week we were studying Algeria to say that Arab women wore veils "because they were dogs." He had a scowl on his face when he said it, which made him look like a dog. I can still see the look on his face at the end of *The Battle of Algiers*, a movie about the Algerian revolution which ends with crowds of women on the march, crying out their rallying cry, an ethereal sound made by beating the tongue up against the roof of the mouth, "ululululululululul." Change on a face is amazing to behold in a student. The lights went on after the film and I looked over at him; he looked stunned. He walked out of the room ululating to himself, trying out the sounds of the women he had referred to as "dogs" the week before. This same student at the end of the semester, searching for a way to say in French that he had learned to express himself better and that he had new thoughts to talk about, used a phrase he learned in an article by Franz Fanon about the changes in Algerian women during the revolution, "Nous nous sommes dévoilés"—"we took off our veils." A reflexive, collective verb.

Moments like this one make me think that speaking a foreign language is, for me and my students, a chance for growth, for freedom, a liberation from the ugliness of our received ideas and mentalities.

Last week we read a novel I didn't really understand, it seemed too simple and I didn't know how I was going to teach it. I assigned an *explication de texte* to Catherine L, a student who came to French through her French Canadian grandmother and her Catholic schooling. *Explication de texte* gets more precious to me as I grow older with literature. I don't think it works the same way in English because Americans don't have the institution of *explication de texte*, the history and sense of ritual that gives the activity its charm and power. In French class we bend over the language, we caress it and we question it, and we come to understand.

In this particular novel, Patrick Modiano's *Remise de peine*, a crime has occurred in the narrator's childhood. We, the readers, don't know what the crime is, but we know that the novel is working its way slowly toward this unspoken event. The narrator is speaking about the strange time in his childhood leading up to the crime; sometimes he speaks in his child voice and sometimes he speaks as an adult remembering.

In the paragraph that my student Catherine L has chosen for her *explication*, the narrator is recounting the way he watched the adults arriving at the house just as he was going to bed:

> *Les autres les rejoindraient au cours de la soirée. Je ne pouvais m'empêcher de les regarder, par les fentes des persiennes de notre chambre, une fois que Blanche-Neige avait éteint la lumière et nous avait souhaité bonne nuit. Ils venaient, chacun à leur tour, sonner à la porte. Je voyais bien leurs visages, sous la lumière vive de l'ampoule du perron. Certains se sont gravés dans ma mémoire pour toujours. Et je m'étonne que les policiers ne m'aient pas interrogé: pourtant les enfants regardent. Ils écoutent aussi.*

The others would join them in the course of the evening. I couldn't help but watch them, through the gaps in the blinds in our room, once Snow White [nickname for their nanny] had turned off the light and wished us good night. One by one they came and rang the doorbell. I saw their faces clearly under the bright light from the bulb on the stoop. Some of these people are engraved in my memory forever. And I'm surprised that the police didn't interrogate me: because children watch. They listen, too.

Catherine L took us through the paragraph like a detective. She showed us how the verbs changed, how the repetitive imperfect of habit ("ils venaient"—they used to come; "Je voyais"—I used to see) gave way to a judicial *passé composé*: the fact, definitive, that those faces are engraved in memory forever ("certains se sont gravés"). Then the present of memory itself, the retrospective moment ("je m'étonne"—I'm surprised). She outlined the themes: the stupidity of the authorities, the policemen, not to know or value the observations of children. Catherine L concluded very simply by giving us the missing sentence, the sentence that explains all the rest. "Children watch," she said, quoting Modiano, "they listen, too." She explained it to us: "What he really means to say is that they write. Children grow up and they write about what they saw and heard."

I was so busy with the administrative details of my day—faculty meeting, advising majors, writing letters, filing reports—that it wasn't until night came that I thought back on that moment from class and had time to savor it. I cried, not sorrowful tears but tears of happiness from discovering something I hadn't known about before. Why was I so moved by what she said? She had put her finger on Modiano's need to catch up with his past, and on his sadness. She had explained to me his sense of a past that can't be erased but which is always incomplete. That's the meaning of the single paragraph she analyzed and also what the whole novel is trying to say. There are truths about the past but there is no authority, no policeman, ready and able to pin them down.

Maybe it was simpler, what moved me. I was thinking about being a child myself and seeing and hearing but not being able to say yet, not having the words for what I saw. Or having them, but no one asked. No one asks the child what is going on, and the child sees, and listens, and engraves those memories and those people one after another in a private language. It's only later—maybe it's too late—that the pain of those memories is brought forward to the present time of writing. *Remise de peine.* In English it means a commuted sentence.

There was the time in Paris when I told Leilani that Jordan almonds were "dragées." I told her a hard "g" instead of a soft "g," so she pronounced it "dragués" (the verb "draguer" means to pick someone up). The saleslady laughed at her. There was the afternoon Micheline's brother came to the house. I heard Micheline ask, "Tu es au courant pour Charles?" I understood, from the context, that "pour" could mean "about," as well as "for," and that Charles was dead. There was the time I argued with my mother about a cut of veal at the Marché des Grands Hommes in Bordeaux. She looked at me strangely. She didn't understand a word I said—I was shouting at her in French.

Halfway through my life I look back. I can't have a memory without it being shot through with French.

When I was an adolescent, French was my storehouse language. I collected secrets in French; I spoke to myself in French. I know now that my passion for French helped me to put off what I needed to say, in English, to the people around me.

I might have stayed in hiding if it weren't for this book— my ambition to finish it forced me to talk to my family. I spoke with my mother, my brother and sister; I heard what they had to say. Sometimes we fought; sometimes we came to new terms. My father was dead. I couldn't talk to him, except in the place I've reserved for him in my head—the bubble. There was one person left I needed to write. In February, 1992, after a draft of my book was finished, I wrote to Mr. D. I apologized for twenty-two years of silence; I tried to thank him for the gifts he had given me—for Paris. I tried to explain the political passion that had excited me in Berkeley; I told him that I used the phrase "capitalist pig" in my last conversation with Louise, that she had taken offense and accused me of not appreciating him. Had she told him? Was he angry? Did he think I didn't appreciate him? I sent him the books I had written on French fascism and Céline, inscribed with thanks. I told him I was taking students to France that summer, that I would like to convey to them the excitement about the city that he conveyed to me on my first trip there in 1970. I told him I hoped it wasn't too late to hear from him.

Mr. D wrote back as soon as he received my letter, on the stationery I remembered. He recalled the name of the hotel my mother and I had stayed at in Paris: L'Hôtel des Deux Continents. He reminded me that he and I had climbed to the top of Notre Dame and studied the gargoyles there. He answered my questions.

"I am glad you were a flaming liberal in your youth," he wrote, "that is the time to revolt and question."

He wrote, "I am happy that you wrote me as you did."

Mr. D sent my letter to Louise. She wrote me. She didn't remember our last phone conversation as well as I did, but she hadn't ratted on me—she never would have tried to come between me and her father. I'd imagined she had, because I'd wanted to steal him away from her—I'd wanted a father all to myself.

For twenty-two years, a story of my own invention had kept me angry at my friend and alienated me from my mentor.

Three months later, I saw Mr. D and Louise again. He invited me to the opening of an exhibit of his art collection at a museum in Minnesota. I stood in the receiving line with hundreds of other people. He looked older, standing at the head of the line, but I recognized him immediately. It occurred to me that he wasn't going to recognize me—I was sixteen the last time he had seen me. When I got to him I told him my name, and we hugged one another. I went into the exhibit room where the Mondrian was hanging—the same painting that had hung in the D living room when I was growing up: there was Louise.

Why did I hide in French? If life got too messy, I could take off into my second world. Writing about it has made me air my suspicions, my anger, my longings, to people for whom it's come as a total surprise. There was a time when I even spoke in a different register in French—higher and excited, I was sliding up to those high notes in some kind of a hyped-up theatrical world of my own making.

Learning French did me some harm by giving me a place to hide. It's not as if there's a straightforward American self lurking under a devious French one, waiting to come out and be authentic. That's nostalgia—or fiction. French isn't just a metaphor, either—it's a skill. It buys my groceries and pays the mortgage. I'm grateful to French, beyond these material gains, for teaching me that there is more than one way to speak, for giving me a role, for being the home I've made from my own will and my own imagination.

All my life, I've used and abused my gift for language. I'm tempted, down to the last page, to wrap things up too neatly in words.

June 1987–September 1992

Note on the Text

In this memoir, I've changed names and slightly altered circumstances of some people and places.

All English translations of Céline are by Ralph Manheim (New Directions Publishers), with the exception of the passage from *Rigadoon*, which I have revised.

The excerpt from Gertrude Stein's *Paris France* is reprinted with the permission of the Estate of Gertrude Stein. The excerpt from Linda Orr's *A Certain X* is reprinted with the permission of L'Epervier Press.

Acknowledgments

I began working on French Lessons in a writing group that has been meeting since spring 1987 in Durham, Chapel Hill, and Cedar Grove, North Carolina. My thanks go first and foremost to the members of that group—Cathy N. Davidson, Jane Tompkins, and Marianna Torgovnick—for their insight and their support, and for their constant challenge: the challenge to communicate outside the ordinary codes of academic language, and to write with feeling.

Crucial financial and material support for my writing came in the form of a Mellon grant at the National Humanities Center during the academic year 1989–90.

For help, inspiration, advice, and encouragement, I am indebted to Amy Allen, Louise Antony, Angelika Bammer, R. Howard Bloch, Anne-Marie Bryan, Tom Clark, Virginia Daley, Lore Dickstein, Morris Dickstein, Spence Foscue, Vivian Foushee, Diana Gilligan, Henri Godard, Janine S. Godard, Valerie Golden, Carolyn Heilbrun, Marianne Hirsch, Denis Hollier, Elizabeth Houlding, Barbara Keyworth, Paula Krist, Lawrence D. Kritzman, Charles Kronberg, Carlton Lake, Gayle Levy, R. W. B. Lewis, Catherine Maggio, Greil Marcus,

Kent Mullikin, Jean O'Barr, Nicholas Raphael, Joseph Rio, Juliette Rogers, Andy Rowland, Chuck Sanislow, Naomi Schor, Ann Smock, the Solstice Assembly (especially our director, Jane Peppler, and the "alto-mobile": Rivka Gordon, Candace Carraway, and Laurie Fox), Margaret Spires, Joan Stewart, Deborah Swain, Jean-Jacques Thomas, Clare Tufts, Barbara Vance, Phil Watts, Susan Weiner, Martha Williams, Carter Wilson.

I wish that Carol Boren Owens were alive to see this book in print.

I am grateful to the Duke students in my 1987 and 1991 graduate and undergraduate seminars on autobiography and to the members of the 1988 Duke-in-Paris summer program—especially Sherri Braden and Jerry Marsini.

Rachel Brownstein, Michèle Farrell, R. W. B. Lewis, Nancy K. Miller, Kristin Ross, Philippe Roussin, and my editor, Alan Thomas, read the entire manuscript at different stages. I benefited enormously from their comments. Laurel Goldman's critical reading of the penultimate draft was invaluable.

Team-teaching with Linda Orr since 1986, on World War II, on war and memory, and on first-person narrative, has informed my thinking and enriched my work in every way. Without our conversations, this book could never have been written.

In Minnesota, my mother, Leonore Yaeger Kaplan, responded to my questions with courage, generosity, and questions of her own. Thank you to my brother, Mark Kaplan, especially for sending me his short story, "Bike Trip to Wildhurst" (1990); to my uncle, Sheldon Kaplan, and to my cousins, Ann Phillips and Felix Phillips, for their hospitality.

Special thanks go to my sister, Hattie Jutagir, for her honesty; her story of our family is different.

To Terry Vance, a teacher in the deepest sense, my gratitude.

French Lessons is dedicated with love and thanks to David Auerbach.

The Author

Alice Kaplan was educated at Berkeley and Yale, and teaches French Literature at Duke University. Her books include *Reproductions of Banality: Fascism, Literature, and French Intellectual Life*.